Intersections

Intersections

Science, Theology, and Ethics

James M. Gustafson

The Pilgrim Press
Cleveland, Ohio

The Pilgrim Press, Cleveland, Ohio 44115
© 1996 by James M. Gustafson

Chapter 2, "Moral Discourse about Medicine: A Variety of Forms," was published in *Journal of Medicine and Philosophy* 15 (1990): 125–42. Copyright © 1990 by *Journal of Medicine and Philosophy, Inc.* Reprinted by permission. Materials drawn upon in the development of this book but not used directly include my chapter, "Theological Anthropology and the Human Sciences," in *Theology at the End of Modernity,* ed. Sheila Greeve Davaney (Philadelphia: Trinity Press International, 1991); permission is gratefully acknowledged.

Printed in the United States of America on acid-free paper

01   00   99   98   97   96   5   4   3   2   1

Library of Congress Cataloging-in-Publication Data
Gustafson, James M.
      Intersections : science, theology, and ethics / James M. Gustafson.
            p.   cm.
      Includes bibliographical references and index.
      ISBN 0-8298-1137-0 (alk. paper)
      1. Christian ethics.   2. Religion and science.
      3. Medical ethics.   I. Title.
      BJ1251.G8765   1996
      241—dc20   96-28322
                                                         CIP

Contents

Preface

Each chapter of this book, except the introduction, was initially prepared in response to a request to make a presentation or contribute an article. The acknowledgments indicate the occasion and the institution, and the fact that permission has been granted to use the material here. Most of the chapters have been previously published. The book is more a collection of essays than a systematic work, though the intersection of disciplines provides a general theme.

The Personal Preface

In 1988 I made a quite radical shift in my professional life, one in which the discontinuities were greater than the continuities. My self-understanding for four decades of scholarship and teaching (including six years of graduate school divided between the Federated Faculty of the University of Chicago and Yale University) was that I was a theologian whose primary area of interest was ethics, but whose interest in ethics required study of disciplines relevant to particular arenas of moral and public choices and actions that attracted my attention. "Cross-disciplinary" activity was present right from the beginning of my academic life: a bachelor of divinity thesis on Max Weber in 1951; a Ph.D. dissertation using concepts from sociology and social theory to examine the relations between what might now be called temporality and a sense of community, with focus on the church; and experiences as a pastor and as a participant in some pioneering ventures of ethics and policy discussions.

Among the latter was participation in a 1956 evaluation of employee relations policies at what was then called Standard Oil of New Jersey. I studied the efficiency reports on twenty-one barges and nine tugboats in the New York Harbor to frame issues of whether cost-reduction proposals for inland transportation of oil products would fit the established, very morally agreeable (but paternalistic) employee-friendly work situation. Also important was my participation in the Institute of Ethics and Politics, established at Wesleyan University by my teacher and friend Kenneth Underwood, which drew participants from active careers in politics and the private sector as well as various academic fields.

The first book review I published was of a volume in the *Ethics and Economic Life* series sponsored by the Federal Council of Churches;[1] it shows a young man's lack of patience, but also a perspective from which I have never moved very far, namely that ethics have to be more complexly engaged in the appropriate social analysis than the statement of "middle axioms" achieves.

While the courses I have taught ranged quite widely, the backbone of my career I viewed to be lectures in theological ethics and seminars in that field for doctoral students. My view has always been that theological ethics, or Christian ethics, were defined by more theological than philosophical literature—biblical, historical, and contemporary—that reasonably fell under that caption. The agenda for studying selections from that literature was framed basically by ways in which theology was related to ethics, and vice versa. My own mature and carefully considered judgments about substantial matters in both the literature and the agenda were not published until 1981 and 1984 in *Ethics from a Theocentric Perspective*, volumes that have been (in the words of Edward Farley) praised with loud damns.[2] Scores of doctoral dissertations I directed or co-advised attended to items on my agenda for the field; few, if any, of them show any significant indication of my own systematic position.

I was invited by a veteran of my Yale seminars, James T. Laney, president of Emory University, to join its faculty in 1988 to conduct a seminar for faculty members from various fields and schools throughout the university. Funding for this seminar came primarily from the Luce Foundation. Up to twelve persons were to be relieved of their teaching and administrative responsibilities to participate (under the most optimal arrangements, this was often modified). I departed somewhat from Emory's proposal by making ethics, per se, less prominent in the themes chosen, which are human being/being human, responsibility, nature, and what I refer to as "describing, explaining, and valuing." Selected participants proposed books appropriate to the topic and my initial agenda for study by all participants. I selected thirteen or fourteen books, each of which was the subject of a critical paper and intense discussion in two seminar sessions per week for two hours each, for one semester. About ninety faculty members participated in the eight years of the Luce program.

The demands of responsible leadership of these Luce Faculty Seminars shifted my use of time and energy from primarily theological ethics and practical moral questions to very broad reading, study, and reflections on the borders and intersections of the various disciplines represented by the readings and participants. I have conducted seminar sessions on more than one hundred different books and read well over three hundred from which we selected those used, ranging from accounts of physical theories to novels and dramas.

If *Ethics from a Theocentric Perspective* appeared to some readers to have involved my move from inside traditional theology to a margin and then a return from that margin, my Emory career has been that in actuality. I continue to be concerned about theology, theological ethics, moral issues, and the church and its ministry, but I confess to not keeping up with as much literature from those fields as I formerly did. However, in almost all of the chapters in this book, I have, in a sense, gone back from a different intellectual and academic place to what had been central for four decades. There is continuity in my intellectual agenda, but it has been revised and somewhat altered.

The materials about which I have to think as a theological ethicist are denser, more diverse, and more complex. Intersections with nontheological materials have always been present in my teaching and much of my writing, but the Emory work in effect makes me move into them less from the standard route of theological ethics. Now I tend to meet theological and ethical materials from the paths of a panorama of academic fields. Indeed, I have formed a deep conviction that theologians and ethicists ought to think most seriously about matters often not attended to in their various professional guilds. Like some others, for example, I have to think about biology theologically and about theology from the standpoint of some matters of biology.

All of the chapters of this book have been drafted since the shift in my professional location. In one sense this book is a more particular focus of an even broader and more general project that involves not only intersections between theology, ethics, and other disciplines, but some other intersections that do not involve theology and ethics. I made an initial presentation of that wider work upon a return visit to the Divinity School of the University of Chicago in 1994, "In the Intersections: Reflections on Being an Academic Traffic Cop."[3]

The Inclusive Intellectual and Cultural Preface

This book is about intersections. It is about the points at which common interests in moral and policy proposals and in intellectual and academic life meet and cross each other, about the paths or roads that intersect at particular points, and about the kinds of disciplinary or perspectival traffic that meet. This book is an inset into a much larger map of intersections, one that includes many points and many disciplines and intellectual perspectives that are not drawn out here, such as how the concern for the natural environment is a point at which various sciences, religious views, ethics, economics, politics, literature and other arts, law and international treaties cross each other. In this book traffic is more limited; it is developed from and applied to basically the intersections of theology, ethics, and some aspects of biology and medicine.

Wayne Booth, in his University of Chicago Ryerson Lecture, "The Idea of a University—as Seen by a Rhetorician," uses the metaphor of islands to interpret contemporary university life; the metaphor is equally applicable to other realms of public activity. He writes, "Must we not admit, then, in all honesty, that we are indeed a pack of ignoramuses, inhabitants of some ancient unmapped archipelago, each of us an island—let John Donne preach as he will—living at a time before anyone had invented boats or any other form of inter-island communication?"[4] Surely this question and the use of the metaphor of islands are appropriate in both academic and public life; they point to the high degree of specialization of research, information, concepts, and terms, of perspectives and modes of argumentation that make it difficult for a literary scholar to understand a book by an economist, or a primatologist to understand a theological book.

Booth's islands are, in my root metaphor, intersections of roads. I presume for good reasons that given a common point of interest, many specializations do intersect, that sometimes the traffic flows smoothly as two or three meet, but at other times virtual gridlock results because of very fundamental differences in interests or in intellectual approaches. Sometimes there is complementarity of description, analysis, and conclusion; sometimes there are severe differences in these processes that require strenuous effort to negotiate.

Several factors motivate the ideas articulated in the individual chapters of this book and in the effort to bring them into a more coherent whole. The first is simply an observation about academic, moral, and public life. There are events, moral and policy issues, research projects in universities, and general conversations in which alternative descriptions of the focal subject exist, alternative concepts and principles of explanation are utilized, alternative interpretations offered, different valuations made of how to account for the subject and how to respond to it, and different wider meanings related to moral, religious, or other interests and perspectives of participants. The example of natural environment is only one of the more obvious cases. Information is drawn from different sources—sometimes highly quantified and sometimes narrative. If recommendations for policy or actions are part of the subject matter, differences in value or moral preferences and commitments meet each other, sometimes to clash, sometimes to compromise, and sometimes to join in concert. And, there are the wider and deeper debates about how our descriptions, concepts, and so on do or do not correspond to the reality of the subject, whether they are or are not social constructions determined by political and ideological as well as other special interests.

In editorials in the daily paper as well as recondite academic treatises about, for example, human nature and activity, there are intersections; choices have been made about what sources, concepts, modes of analysis, arguments, and conclusions are most adequate. The intersections simply are—they exist. The most comprehensive agenda of this project is applicable to many more points than are addressed in its chapters.

There are academic reasons for this project. It assumes, as Wayne Booth does, that in universities and other human communities coming to some mutual understanding is a *conditio sine qua non*. Without a huge commitment to a principle, such as "truth about *x* is one," some academicians, at least, strive to grasp more adequate knowledge and understanding of the subject of the intersection, to explore what insight, information, or principles various academic disciplines contribute, and to adjudicate critically the differences between them in order to evaluate each. Particular intersections require rather precise and "thick" examinations— for example, why and how do different anthropologists differ in their explanations and interpretations of the potlatch ceremony? Why does an economist believe the anthropologists have missed the point, and how is the economic argument made?[5] Increment in mutual understanding among persons or groups with different specialized approaches or different interests and ideologies is a very powerful motive or end, at least to the author of this book.

This is a vision or aspiration for universities, but also for other communities in which different discourses are used about similar phenomena or the same phenomenon. The contention between different approaches, the traffic from different roads, has significant value. It exposes strengths and weaknesses of different contributions; it sharpens self-critical efforts on the part of participants; it contributes to a more comprehensive interpretation of the phenomena under examination. The aspiration is not for the establishment of a leader of the disciplines in a university, for a theory of everything, though agreement on some more generalizable principles is a worthy goal. One does not expect contributors to resign from their fields, or even necessarily to radically modify their approaches. Nor does one aspire for the establishment of "interdisciplinary" work to become a new specialized discipline. Rather, informed and rigorous interaction that can be mutually edifying intellectually is, I take it, what makes an institution approximate its traditional name, "university."

In this book I assume that the same, or a similar, vision or aspiration is applicable in other social and institutional contexts than a university. Communities of religious and moral thought and activity can become uncritically or defensively isolated even from information, ideas, and arguments that impinge upon their self-understandings and their determinations of courses of activity within their communities and in relation to others. Like academic persons, religious leaders and laypeople are exposed to and participate in a variety of languages, concepts, and sources of information about their life choices, what is worthy of belief and what is not, how various languages and frames of reference conflict, complement each other, or mutually exclude each other. Where traffic from other roads is blocked or diverted by a religious community, some reasons have to be given; where there is some melding or where there is critical appropriation of some of the traffic, some intellectual argument has to be made. Religious life and thought is not an island, though for some persons this would appear to be the preferred metaphor; it is, willy-nilly, an intersection that needs vigorous intellectual exploration.

In addition to the academic motives for this project is a deeply practical or moral motive. When the intersection is a moral or policy issue, better informed and wiser choices on the part of individual or institutional agents are more likely to occur when traffic crosses from a variety of roads. The possibility of gridlock is present, however, here as at more narrowly intellectual points. For example, the physicist Robert Sachs and I conducted periodic faculty seminars on the ethics of nuclear deterrence in the last years of the cold war, with the aspiration that participants might come to some agreement not only on the large subjects, such as avoidance of armed conflict, but also on policies involving denser particular choices, such as various arms control treaties, enforcement policies, and political supports. While mutual understanding was achieved, to some extent, between physicists, Sovietologists, international relations experts, philosophers, theologians, and others, in the end much deeper consensus was frustrated by disagreements about which information, which concepts, which modes of argumentation should be central and ultimately govern other sources and their uses. A Kantian-based argument that if it is immoral to use nuclear weapons it is immoral to threaten to use them could be understood as an argument, but be rejected by participants who believed that military and political information and analysis should be primary. Analyses of what is going on, rather than what ought not to be done, was primary for them.

An example of limited success on a terribly complex issue, however, does not deter the conviction that there are practical moral reasons for closer, more refined analysis of intersections in various policy or moral issues. Even to defend a moral position, such as limited use of genetic research for moral reasons, requires a comprehension of why broader use might be judged morally wrong.

Activists sometimes object that multiple analysis leads to moral paralysis, and that various interests and powers can use different analyses in their own interests. They have a point. The public cannot avoid seeing how different institutional or ideological interests develop statistical studies of the same issues, and support their positions on the basis of the sciences enlisted. With this caveat, however, I judge the importance of having the most accurate information and most careful analyses and arguments to be more responsible than to assert moral and social policy positions on the basis of deep moral or ideological convictions alone.

This book takes the task of examining intersections as its agenda not only for academic and more narrowly intellectual reasons, but for the sake of more prudent development of actions. The theological argument and position developed in volume 1 of my *Ethics from a Theocentric Perspective* and the ethical position developed there and more fully in volume 2 virtually entail a very high priority for the agenda of this book. If, as I argue in those volumes, participation in patterns and process of interdependence in the world of nature, in human interactions, and in social and cultural life is the most general characteristic of the world in which we live, descriptions, explanations, and interpretations of those patterns and processes—in the very particularities of what goes on between me and my garden, our life together in marriage and family, and the political and economic relations between nation states—cannot avoid the intersections of variant sources. If, as I also argue, in the context of religious piety those patterns and processes are interpreted as an ordering by the Divine, an understanding of them has to be taken into account very centrally in articulating the meaning of the Divine. What one says theologically has to be informed, necessarily, by our best knowledge of these patterns and processes. And if the moral imperative that follows is to relate to all things as we can understand their relations to the divine ordering, the values, rules, and principles that direct human action have a basis in the knowledge gained about the roads and their intersections.

Theologically and ethically my work is a form of "naturalism." The chapters of this book do not develop this fundamental stance philosophically or theologically. My observation at this point is simply this: Some forms of both theology and ethical theory are developed and articulated so that their premises are not as dependent upon scientific and historical accounts of how things really are; in their application to interpreting the meaning of human events religiously and morally, and in giving some counsel or directives to the agents, however, they do intersect with accounts of other relevant disciplines—economics, biology, medicine, and others. One has theologies and ethics that apply to or use information from various disciplines and forms of analysis, but are not themselves in any way altered by this information and explanation. The traffic in their intersections with other ideas and information flows in one direction—from the theology or ethical theory to an account of the subject to which it is applied or is interpreted by it. In the case of my work (and that of others as well), traffic goes both ways at the intersections of theology and ethics, with accounts of what is going on, which are derived from other sources; it affects how theology and ethics are described and interpreted. This is addressed indirectly and directly in several of the chapters of this book.

Like many of my earlier articles and books, these chapters have a pedagogical intention, namely to show readers alternative approaches to various intersections, and what follows from taking one or another of them. These chapters both follow from, in some ways, the systematic work of *Ethics from a Theocentric Perspective*, and continue the more comparative analytic genre of earlier books. My own preferences are indicated and to some extent defended and developed in various chapters, but they do not advance a normative position as their primary intention. I reiterate, however, the importance of analyzing the interactions chosen for this book and of pressing readers to take account of the analyses grounded in *Ethics from a Theocentric Perspective*.

Acknowledgments

The material in this book is drawn from lectures and articles prepared in response to requests from various persons and institutions since my transition from a professorship in theological ethics to one called "Humanities and Comparative Studies" in 1988. Some of the chapters are changed very little from earlier versions; others draw upon previously published and unpublished presentations in more revised ways. Permission has been granted to use in whole or draw from the following.

CHAPTER 1, "Explaining and Valuing the Human: An Inevitable Theological and Scientific Encounter," presented as the University Lecture in Religion at Arizona State University, February 1990, was published by its Department of Religious Studies in booklet form in that year.

CHAPTER 2, "Moral Discourse about Medicine: A Variety of Forms," was published in *Journal of Medicine and Philosophy* 15 (1990): 125–42. Copyright ©1990 by *Journal of Medicine and Philosophy, Inc.* Reprinted by permission.

CHAPTER 3, "Styles of Religious Reflection in Medical Ethics," was presented at the Institute of Religion, Texas Medical Center, Houston, October 23, 1993, at a conference on theology and medical ethics.

Chapter 4, "Genetic Therapy: An Intersection of Science, Ethics, and Theology," is derived from a lecture presented at the National Cathedral, Washington, D.C., September 30, 1991, upon invitation by Canon Michael Hamilton. The lecture was published by the National Cathedral as Cathedral Papers #4, "A Christian Perspective on Genetic Engineering," in 1992.

Chapter 5, "Theology, Biology, and Ethics: Further Explorations," is adapted from a lecture, "Theologians and Geneticists," delivered at the Institute of Religion, Texas Medical Center, Houston, March 14, 1992, at a conference titled "Implications of the Human Genome Project for Medicine, Theology, Ethics, and Policy," under DOE Grant No. DE-FG05-91ER 61181.

Chapter 6, "Human Viability: To What End?," is adapted from a lecture, "Human Viability: A Western Religious and Ethical Response," delivered in Chicago on November 16, 1991, at a Templeton Symposium titled "Human Viability and a World Theology," sponsored by the Chicago Center for Religion and Science.

Chapter 7, "Conclusion: The Relation of Other Disciplines to Theological Ethics," is developed from a paper presented to a plenary session of the Society of Christian Ethics, in Chicago, January 1994, at the invitation of Professor Margaret Farley.

Materials drawn upon in the development of this book but not used directly include my chapter, "Theological Anthropology and the Human Sciences," from *Theology at the End of Modernity*, edited by Sheila Greeve Davaney (Philadelphia: Trinity Press International, 1991); permission is gratefully acknowledged. Lecture materials out of which that chapter and portions of this book were developed include "Human Being/Being Human," the Ecumenical Chair Lecture, Xavier University, Cincinnati, Ohio, October 1989, and "The Human: Where the Humanities and the Sciences Meet," delivered at several institutions during 1990–91 as a Phi Beta Kappa Visiting Scholar.

At various stages of development of the chapters and the book as a whole I received many beneficial critical comments, some of which I have taken into account, from many persons, including Robert Audi, William Schweiker, Leslie Griffin, Robert McCauley, Harlan Beckley, Margaret Farley, William French, Stephen Pope, Diane Yeager, Jean Porter, anonymous reviewers for journals, and oral commentators in public gatherings. Special gratitude goes to Martin Cook, my empathetic critic for many years, whose criticism of an earlier draft of the whole book led to drastic revisions and finally to his approval; to Ann Temkin, my secretary and assistant in the Luce Seminar program at Emory, whose reading led to rearrangement and deletions that benefit the book, and who did the final typing; to Sylvia Everett, who preceded Ann Temkin and typed and corrected more than once, I believe, everything included and much discarded. Louise, my beloved wife for forty-nine years, encouraged me when I despaired of ever getting this book up to a standard of quality I could live with. Richard Brown of Pilgrim Press tolerated my delays with great patience. Of course, it would have been a better, or at least very different, book if I could have integrated more of the worthy critical analysis I received from diverse persons. In the end it is authentically my own, whatever faults and merits it contains.

Introduction

The intersections attended to in this book are those at which theology and ethics, and often more particularly theological ethics, meet some sciences. Therefore, it is worthwhile briefly to suggest differing patterns of traffic that are further addressed in these chapters. One variant of pattern is that of the *authority* of theology, ethical theory, and theological ethics. Just as the Kantian-inspired paper on the immorality of a threat to use nuclear weapons assumed a privileged position for ethical theory as the starting and defining point for a seminar on ethics of deterrence, so some positions in theology and theological ethics claim independence and privilege.

One basis for this is that theology or theological ethics have authority independent of particular premises of descriptions, explanations, and interpretations of events which they address, for example, medical procedures and research, political proposals, or policy recommendations about the environment. The authorization of the theology and ethics, in this stance, is not "naturalistic"; it is (in its strongest claim) that a special revelation of God is given in the Scriptures and/or through the tradition. The revelation is independent from other knowledge and other modes of knowing. It can be applied to events and phenomena to give them a different explanation, to direct human action, and to indicate the ultimate outcome of all things. Examples of this are "creationist science" and the use of particular biblical passages to condemn homosexuality.

The same privilege, however, is implied in more subtle and sophisticated theological ethics. For example, the widely accepted notion that love constitutes the defining feature of Christian ethics, backed by the authority of the biblical narratives in both parts of the Bible, functions in a somewhat similar way. This love, however it is delineated, is applied in ideational form or in practice to interactions with events as complex as war and economic ordering. The traffic flows in one direction; nothing informed by any sciences or other perspectives can change the independent authority of love as the central norm for Christians. Love is applied to what is analyzed militarily, economically, or biologically to direct appropriate action.

Another basis for a claim of privilege for theology or theological ethics is that they provide a *more comprehensive way* to interpret events that are described and explained by traffic coming from other disciplinary routes. They enlarge what is relevant in understanding more comprehensively the depth or ultimate "meaning" of the events and phenomena, explained in nontheological terms. Certain features that are omitted or insufficiently accounted for by other traffic in an intersection become exposed; this is often justified because of the reductionistic tendencies of other approaches. For example, biology and physiology can explain the processes of dying due to a variety of causes, but they do not address the dimensions of meaning, ultimacy, and breadth of context that humans experience in dying or in relation to the dying of others. Theology does.

The claim of privilege here is often justified by a valuable outcome of the traffic from theology and theological ethics. An example is the affirmation, which Christian faith and theology assure humans, that hope and the possibility of redemption always lie beyond the starkness of tragedy.

No events in history or personal experience can assail this, since it is part of God's revelation. The outcome of an interpretation of events in the light of this belief is always to stress the possibilities of good coming out of evil, of openness within apparent restraints and restrictions of possibilities. This can issue in remedies for personal and social despair, as well as offering courses of action when possibilities from other perspectives appear to be blocked.

A third basis of a claim for privilege can be distinguished: theology, theological ethics, or ethics offer the most important approaches to events and phenomena because the *most critical issues* in them and in any interpretation of them *are religious and moral*. Thus the concepts, metaphors, and narratives of these approaches or disciplines ought to override the interpretations of others, subordinate the functions of others to the theological or ethical interpretation, or integrate them into a coherent theological or ethical framework because of their preeminent importance. This basis of a claim does not, in the contemporary world, rest on an arrogant assertion that theology is the ruler of the sciences. Rather it is grounded in deep convictions that at the bottom of policy disputes the most important questions are ethical, at the heart of interpretations of human nature and activity the most important questions are theological, such as the relation of the human to the Divine or the Transcendent, if not to the God of Abraham, Isaac, and Jacob and the God and father of Jesus Christ. The conviction that the most critical issues are always religious and moral gives privilege to the concepts, symbols, and narratives of ethics and theology.

In this basis as well, the traffic tends to flow through the intersection in one direction, that is from the ethical and theological into other sources of information and concepts. One might find happy complementarity between, for example, a particular scientific account and a theological one, such as when the physical theory of an open universe seems coherent with a theological conviction that God makes all things new. Or, by affirming the priority of the concepts, metaphors, and narratives of theology and ethics, one might find that certain evidence from other sources have to be ignored or in some way reduced in their potential moral and religious significance. An example is an ethical position that is grounded in a view of radical human freedom; this freedom has to be defined and defended in such a way that inferences drawn from biopsychology or genetics do not qualify the necessary capacity for full personal responsibility for actions.

More congenial to my own views, as developed in earlier publications and to some extent in this book, is a claim to participate and be taken into account, with the open possibility that the theology and ethical theory will be informed and even altered by concepts, information, and theories that they meet at particular intersections. In any dialectical intersection informed by relevant disciplines and experiences, theology, ethics, and theological ethics can and should be included. The justification is not based on some independent external authorization. It might be supported by many current views of the partiality and limitations of various disciplines and experiences, thus affirming that no ruler of the discourse has been crowned. To base participation on that, however, smacks of defensiveness; other disciplines are not absolute in their findings and authorizations, and neither are theology and ethics.

Therefore theology and ethics have a claim to be heard as much as other views. (This is the actual defense of "creation science" in public discourse.) My point is that even within the religious communities theological ethics and theology engage in intersections, the outcome of which is determined not simply by their traffic, but by a different mixture of sources of information, concepts, and modes of argument. The outcome of an interpretation, moral choice, or policy discussion is informed, but not necessarily determined, by theology or ethics. As noted in the preface, my systematic account of *Ethics from a Theocentric Perspective* supports this general stance.

Intersections are specific. Theology or theological ethics intersect different disciplines depending on the interest of the scholar or writer. Different levels of generalization also come into consideration. If the interest is primarily in questions of method, the theologian meets philosophical issues of epistemology, and often engages in discourse comparable to that of philosophers of science. Truth claims for theology are compared with those for other investigations. The aim is to provide some justification for the truth or meaningfulness claims of religious discourse. A theological interest directed toward methods of Christian ethics meets various ethical theories developed by philosophers and others; the upshot might be essays on the function of rules in Christian ethics.

One's interest might be in particular doctrines; depending on which doctrine, information and concepts from different sciences are met. For example, in *Treasure in Earthen Vessels: The Church as a Human Community,* my interest was primarily in the doctrine or the nature of the church.[1] Because of the contemporary interest in the church in commissions of the ecumenical movement, my studies of sociology and social theory, and some experiences as a pastor, I sought to develop an interpretation which, like some of the work of my mentor, H. Richard Niebuhr, took more seriously the human institutional aspects of church life—its social, political, and historical dimensions. What could be explained or interpreted in traditional theological terms could also be explained and interpreted in terms of sociology and social theory. The phenomenon, the church, could be analyzed from different perspectives; one option at the intersection was to propose a religious significance and meaning to processes and structures that were explicable in naturalistic terms.

If the interest is primarily in descriptions, explanations, and interpretations of the human—in other words, in theological or moral anthropology—the scholar intersects not only with alternative philosophical but also various scientific accounts. Various nontheological disciplines issue in diverse interpretations of the phenomenon; these can be judged to be partial or to have very comprehensive explanatory powers. They may flow smoothly with a theological course of traffic or obstruct it.

Polarities abound in the history of discussion of the human: nature and nurture; spirit, mind, and body; brain and consciousness; freedom and determinism; the human and nonhuman; biology and culture, to name only a few. In our time the borders between these distinctions are described somewhat differently from earlier discussions. To be sure, the issue of freedom versus determinism continues to be critical, but the context for the theologian and ethicist is denser because of information and interpretations from various psychological theories, various points of view in modern anthropology—economic, biosocial, symbolic interaction, and others. Feminists, geneticists, and others offer critiques of traditional resolutions of issues and provide new proposals. Because theology and ethics, as well as historical and other intellectual inquiries, assume premises about the human, the information, concepts, interpretations, and explanations have to be taken into account in some way. Further discussion of this occurs in subsequent chapters.

One's interest might be in the doctrine of God. For centuries some interpretations of God have been informed not only by biblical or other specific religious traditions but also by contemporary philosophies and sciences, such as the deism of the eighteenth century. The sciences that theology meets with this interest are likely to be different from those confronted most directly when anthropology is the focus. And one finds scientists who engage in the theological speculations on the basis of contemporary theories. For example, a theologian, Jürgen Moltmann in *God in Creation*, and a scientist who engages in speculative cosmology (with religious undertones), Freeman Dyson in *Infinite in All Directions*, adduce inferences from physical theory about the infinitely expanding universe to warrant theological (in fact or in spirit) proposals about an open future and thus a ground of hope. Philip Hefner, in *The Human Factor*,[2] is equally interested in interpreting God and nature as God's great project; he turns to biological more than physical theories to find coherence between scientific and some traditional Christian sources and themes.

If the interest is moral, the intersection will be determined by the courses of information and theories that seem reliably to account for the circumstances or events in which a moral choice is to be made. Sometimes several disciplines that meet each other also meet theology and ethics where policy is at issue—again, remember environmental concerns. At other times the account of what is going on, which sets out alternative courses of action for a moral choice, is more limited, for example, in certain clinical medical situations.

These matters are developed in various ways in some of the chapters of this book. This outline of the framework of wider interests that shape the discussions is intended to provide direction and incentive for further pursuit not only of what is in this book but beyond it in various directions.

The acknowledgments list the sources of previously published and unpublished forms of the following chapters, and the fact that permission was granted for their use here. In some instances the form taken in this book is a conflation of materials published or developed in lectures. Because each of the ensuing chapters was initially developed in response to an invitation to write and/or lecture, it is appropriate to say a bit about those occasions and how they affected what I wrote for them.

Chapter 1, "Explaining and Valuing the Human," came more directly out of sessions of the first Luce Faculty Seminar at Emory University. The invitation to lecture under the auspices of a Department of Religious Studies at a state university, Arizona State, made an appropriate occasion to look somewhat precisely (but less so than is possible with the materials used) at how similar life outlooks are backed by radically different sources of information, concepts, and arguments. Both Reinhold Niebuhr's *Nature and Destiny of Man* and Melvin Konner's *The Tangled Wing* were subjects of critical papers and intensive discussion in the first seminar; indeed, Konner wrote the critical paper on Niebuhr. The chapter could induce similar comparative studies, including writings that use largely common sources of information, concepts, and modes of argumentation about the human and come to radically different life outlooks.

Chapters 2 through 5 attend, in one way or another, to intersections of ethics, medicine, and theology. Although I have not been intensely involved in the discussions of medical ethics in recent years, various editors and organizers of conferences elicited sufficient interest for me to reflect upon topics currently under examination. For the purpose of this book, these chapters are primarily examples of intersections of disciplines, or ways of working and writing; any contribution they make to medical ethical discussions is of secondary importance.

The second chapter was written at the request of two philosophers who edited an issue of *The Journal of Medicine and Philosophy* that addressed retrospectively how the field of medical ethics got where it is and how. In this chapter I use a pattern developed in the Henry Stob Lectures at Calvin College and Theological Seminary to analyze literature about medicine that is morally relevant, if not ethical in the strictest disciplinary sense. I believe that pattern can be heuristically useful with political, economic, and other types of literature that propose analysis and recommend actions. Indeed, I have used it to some extent in *A Sense of the Divine*, my short foray into environmental discussions.[3]

Chapter 3 was developed for a conference that specifically addressed whether theology and religious thought still contributed to medical ethics. I used the occasion to form a typology of ways that traffic has been directed where these interests or fields meet. The chapter functions as a heuristic device for reflection both on literature and oral practice by religious medical ethicists; indeed, a common response to the presentation affirmed my conclusion, namely that each of the types developed is used by the same persons depending on the context being addressed, or in which they are interacting with other literature or persons.

The fourth chapter developed as a result of Canon Michael Hamilton's invitation to participate in an evening of presentations and discussion with Dr. French Anderson at the National Cathedral in Washington, D.C. This brought me back into examination of new developments in genetic science and their applications, something I had attended to more systematically two decades earlier. Since Anderson had written on ethics, I focused first on how he developed his ethical arguments and then raised some larger issues, particularly the vexing one of the relation between our descriptive and normative or valuative views of the human, a matter I also had addressed decades before.[4] That issue continues to be implicit as often as it is explicit in scientific and philosophical accounts developed on the basis of genetics, neurobiology, psychology, economics, and other fields, as well as accounts in theology, ethics, and literature that affirm a normative position more explicitly. The issue is not only intellectually intriguing as one examines it in various writings; various positions have implications for how moral accountability and religious experiences are interpreted and defended.

Chapter 5 further explores some of the themes of previous chapters, and particularly chapter 4. It was initially developed for a conference that deliberately engaged theologians with genetic researchers and therapists, including Dr. French Anderson. More than in some other chapters, recent theological publications are drawn into my analysis of the places where theology, genetics and biology, and ethics meet.

Chapter 6 was composed initially for a conference from which comes its title, "Human Viability." The content is more theological than ethical in focus and certainly reflects the theocentric perspective more systematically presented in the two volumes of my *Ethics*.

Chapter 7 was written at the invitation of Professor Margaret Farley for the opening plenary session of the Society of Christian Ethics meeting in January 1994. Its function there was to turn my closest professional colleagues' attention to the theme of this book, namely the intersections of other fields with theological ethics. Various critical responses, with recommendations for its revision, were sent to me, none of which led to its publication anywhere. The form it takes here is a summary and, with further refinement, a conclusion to the previous chapters.

Explaining and Valuing the Human: An Inevitable Theological and Scientific Encounter

The human is an intersection at which many disciplines, arts, and practices cross. Rather than focus on the most general issues, this chapter focuses primarily on two influential books.

Theologians, moral philosophers, scientists, novelists and dramatists, and others engage in descriptions, explanations, interpretations, and valuations of human life. Such inquiries have probably occupied as much attention from individuals seeking to make sense of their suffering (its causes and its meaning or significance) as from theorists with quite different academic specializations. Books abound on the subject, including books that seek to order different theories of the human as they have been proposed historically, cross-culturally, scientifically, and religiously. Traditionally, religion and more speculative philosophy as well as literature and art have attended to the value and meaning of human life, to the different contexts in which value and meaning are to be found or proposed, and for some, to the edification of human persons so that their potential values are fulfilled.

Side by side with this, and sometimes integrated into it, are descriptions of the "essence" of the human, the features that distinguish the human from other forms of life. "Humanists" as well as "scientists," both before such distinctions were made and since, have proffered not only descriptions, but also explanations and interpretations of the nature and activity of humans. The inquiry is ancient, and it continues in many genres of writing and art. Its pervasiveness is suggested in opening sentences of two works that are central to the analysis in this chapter, as well as in other sources.

Reinhold Niebuhr begins his classic Gifford Lectures, *The Nature and Destiny of Man*, with these sentences: "Man has always been his own most vexing problem. How shall he think of himself?" Bioanthropologist Melvin Konner begins the "Prefatory Inquiry" to his study *Biological Constraints on the Human Spirit*, the subtitle of his book *The Tangled Wing*, as follows: "Why we are what we are, why we do what we do, why we feel what we feel: these questions have been on the minds of philosophers and theologians, medical men and medicine men, actors, diplomats, poets and, of course, scientists, beginning with the first glimmer of human thought itself." By way of contrast, compare Carl Degler's *In Search of Human Nature*, which opens with a quotation from Margaret Mead: "'What must we do to be human?' is a question as old as humanity itself."[1] The quotations from Niebuhr and Konner are analytically oriented; the one from Mead is more normative. As we shall see, those authors who begin with analysis also develop answers to Mead's question, and those who propose what we ought to be and do rely upon descriptions, explanations, and interpretations of the human that cohere with and support their answers in the "ought" question.

Inquiries into the human address various levels of generalization or abstraction. On one level the issue is logical as well as moral, that is, what are the relations between the facts about the human to the values of the human, between indicative and imperative language, between the "is" and the "ought" of the human? This still-controverted issue is important, but it becomes more complex and more interesting when one examines these relations in denser and more fully developed accounts by persons interested in each of the poles, and by creative authors and others.

One of the debates currently going on among feminist authors is the relation between the biological "isness," or distinctiveness of women, to what constitutes their well-being and rights. The same issue is equally present in thinking about male sexuality. Persons who begin with the "ought" have explicit or implied descriptions and explanations of the human that support their claims to its value and meaning. Feminists, for example, who back their moral and policy proposals with arguments that are rooted in the early modern traditions of "individualistic liberalism," discount the distinctive biological functions of women as less important than do some others.[2]

I proceed to the principals of this chapter, Niebuhr and Konner, with another introductory comparison. Rabbi Abraham Heschel in his book *Who Is Man?* basically argues that *who* we are should guide and determine *what* we are or what we are to become. What it means to be human should determine what human beings become. But, he says, "there is the ontological connective between human being and being human," that is, between what we essentially are and what we ought to be and become:

> Man's being human [the more normative pole] is consti-
> tuted by his essential sensibilities, by his modes of re-
> sponse to the realities he is aware of—to the being that *I*
> am, to the beings that surround *me*, to the being that
> transcends *me*—or, more specifically, by how he relates
> to the existence that he is, to the existence of his fellow

men, to what is given in his immediate surroundings, to
that which *is* but is not immediately given.[3]

The normative, being human, "is inherent as a desideratum in human being," that is, in what constitutes our
being. Heschel is interested in "who" we are, but that is inherent in "what" we are. Thus his description of what we
are is susceptible to investigation for the accuracy, or adequacy, of its empirical and explanatory bases. And, interestingly, he says that "we can attain adequate understanding of man only if we think of man in human terms . . . and
abstain from employing categories developed in the investigation of lower forms of life."[4]

I infer from this that Heschel believes we are to abstain
from using concepts and explanations from genetics and
other aspects of biology in our effort to attain an adequate
understanding of the human and the meaning of being
human. Heschel does not eliminate a description, but he
limits what is to be taken into account in one because he
wants to focus on what is *distinctively* or *uniquely* human.
The uniquely human, however, can be described biologically, as well.

Just as a theological or humanistic account relies on a
description, if not an explanation, of the human, so many
writers from the human sciences move from explanation to
what is to be valued about human life and to its meaning.
On Human Nature, by sociobiologist Edward O. Wilson, can
be used to illustrate this. Wilson, I must acknowledge,
states that his book is not strictly scientific, but it is clear
that he desires to support his more expansive view of the
human with as much evidence and theory from various
sciences as he can muster.

Early on Wilson summarizes the essence of the argument, "that the brain exists because it promotes the survival
and multiplication of the genes that direct its assembly. The
human mind is a device for survival and reproduction, and

reason is just one of its various techniques." In an earlier, more strictly scientific work, he provided critics with an oft-cited comment, "The organism is only DNA's way of making more DNA."[5] Note what is in the service of what. The human mind is in the service of survival and reproduction, not reproduction in the service of the mind. Reason is a technique for survival; it is not in the service of the calling of the human to use reason. The organism is in the service of DNA, not DNA in the service of the organism. Here we see how explanations of human life support quite specific valuations of its importance.

Wilson closes his account of human nature with a chapter titled "Hope," the details of which I will not develop, except to explain that the human species finally faces a "spiritual dilemma" that leads Wilson to give a kind of evangelical moral call: "The human species can change its own nature. What will it choose? Will it remain the same, teetering on a jerrybuilt foundation of partly obsolete Ice-Age adaptations? Or will it press on toward still higher intelligence and creativity, accompanied by a greater—or lesser—capacity for emotional response?" And the final peroration is,

> The true Promethean spirit of science means to liberate man by giving him knowledge and some measure of dominion over the physical environment. But at another level, and in a new age, it also constructs the mythology of scientific materialism, guided by the corrective devices of the scientific method, addressed with precise and deliberately affective appeal to the deepest needs of human nature, and kept strong by the blind hope that the journey on which we are now embarked will be further and better than the one just completed.[6]

Heschel, you recall, says we are to abstain from precisely that on which Wilson bases his account, "categories developed in the investigation of lower forms of life." But

Heschel also says that the meaning and value of the human are inherent as a desideratum in what we are. On that general point, I think, our two authors formally agree. Their outlooks (and I deliberately use a very general term) are, however, very opposed. One critical factor is the difference in their descriptions of the human. And a critical question is whether Heschel has given us a description for the sake of supporting a normative view. Similarly, does Wilson's call at the end follow necessarily from his description and explanation, or has he some elided premises?

This example illustrates the systematic questions that are the center of this chapter. How are descriptions and explanations of the human related to valuations and meanings of the human? Or, conversely, what descriptions and explanations do persons primarily interested in making a case for the value and meaning of the human provide to back their more normative purposes? These questions could be pursued with attention to a vast scholarly literature, both historical and current. In this chapter I offer a more intensive analysis of Niebuhr's *The Nature and Destiny of Man* and Konner's *The Tangled Wing: Biological Constraints on the Human Spirit.* The chapter is more one of exploration and critical analysis than a constructive conclusion. An intuition, and not merely a private one, is that these two treatises issue in somewhat similar dispositions or outlooks toward life in the world: a realism that avoids despair on the one hand and avoids secure confidence on the other. This similarity makes my choice particularly interesting.

The structure of the rest of this chapter is as follows. First I will indicate evidence for my conclusion that these two treatises propose somewhat similar purposes and outcomes. Examples, which will be developed later, are the rhetorical intention to increase human self-understanding, to have this self-understanding as one element in guiding action, and the sense of constraints on human life due to the power of evil. Second, I will analyze the descriptions and explanations of human life and action in each of the treatises, noting the evidence used, the symbols or concepts that are keys to interpretation of the evidence, and the relations of explanations to valuations, or of valuations to explanations. A brief assessment will be made of the coherence of each treatise. Third, I shall move back from the analysis to ask what is at issue between an avowedly theological interpretation and an avowedly scientific one. The answers to that question will further the broader inquiry into other intersections.

Reinhold Niebuhr, a Protestant theologian, delivered the Gifford Lectures in Edinburgh more than fifty years ago. Their publication has probably become one of the most widely studied books by an American religious thinker in this century. But Niebuhr was a theologian motivated by political, social, and moral issues, and thus in the profoundest sense a moral theologian. His treatise is written primarily in traditional Christian language and is clearly addressed most directly to the Christian community.

Melvin Konner is an anthropologist whose field research was done in Southern Africa and whose interests focus on the relations between behavior and biology. He contributes widely to public discussions of medicine, education, health policy, and clinical issues. Konner is also, in a nonpejorative sense, a moralist. He is clearly concerned about human well-being, about the fate of the earth, and as the subtitle of the book under examination shows, the human spirit. His audience is not religious communities, but culturally and scientifically informed publics. His text is laced with insightful use of a variety of creative literature, but its language is overwhelmingly that of the various sciences that explain human being. From what is clearly, in the end, a profound moral concern, he examines the implications of a vast body of scientific literature in a remarkably synthetic way.

These scholars have in common a rhetorical (in a non-pejorative, classic sense) intention. Both see grave threats to human well-being, one during the international, political, and economic events in the middle decades of this century, and the other in the conditions of its last decades. In the face of the threats each, I believe, is concerned to provide evidence and interpretations of human life that enlarge and deepen human self-understanding. Each believes that a more adequate understanding of human nature, or the human condition, will lead to better attitudes and stances toward actual and potential events, and to wiser approaches to human conduct and affairs. Neither, in the treatises under examination in this chapter, engages in recommendations or prescriptions for actual public policy or for personal and interpersonal conduct, though both do in other publications. Their aims here are deeper; a proper interpretation of human being will effect a more adequate orientation to our participation in the processes and patterns of life in the world. The sources each interprets are different, but the outcomes are both interestingly similar and importantly different.

In the preface to the 1941 edition of the first volume of *The Nature and Destiny of Man,* Niebuhr states that his work "is based upon the conviction that there are resources in the Christian faith for understanding human nature which have been lost in modern culture" (1:vii). He views scientific interpretations of human nature to be rooted in definite philosophical presuppositions, which are either "idealistic" or "naturalistic." The idealistic err in overestimating human rational capacities and underestimating the intimate relation between the human spirit and its physical organism. The naturalistic err in not distinguishing between capacities for transcendence from imbeddedness in nature. They explain in biological terms what can, from Niebuhr's perspective, be understood only as a "curious compound of 'nature' and 'spirit'" (1:viii). The task he undertakes, then, is to develop a description and explanation of human nature; he draws upon sources in the Bible and theology, the history of Western culture, and contemporary writings in shaping his argument. These sources offer ideas, theories, and concepts, not empirical scientific evidence.

Konner is adept at drawing upon literary sources for insight, but he argues that an adequate description and explanation of human nature must take into account and build upon biological research. One can paraphrase Niebuhr's conviction: Konner's is that there are resources in the human sciences and particularly in biology for understanding human nature and that these must be the basis for addressing issues of modern culture. Konner's work falls under Niebuhr's category of naturalism, but, on the face of it, his invoking of the human spirit avoids the excesses that Niebuhr sees in that general view. Whether Konner's chapters of analysis *necessarily* lead to his chapter of peroration, or only permit it, is a question to which I shall return.

In that final chapter Konner views the hallmark of our species to be the sense of wonder that is the central feature of the human spirit (435). He suspects that at the present stage of human evolution "the human spirit is insufficiently developed," and he sees the full reinstatement of the sense of wonder as a condition for sustaining and developing the spirit. "We must," he writes, "try once again to experience the human soul as soul, and not just a buzz of bioelectricity; the human will as will, and not just a surge of hormones; the human heart not as a fibrous, sticky pump, but as the metaphoric organ of understanding." These do not need to be "metaphysical entities," as Niebuhr's term *spirit* suggests, but the words we have to use to talk about them make them "unassailable, even though they are dissected before our eyes" (435–36).

To all this, Niebuhr might retort that his idea of spirit, which locates human capacities to transcend embodiment, is more than a sense of wonder, and that even the loss of that sense is fostered by the dominance of a biological naturalistic account of life. He might agree with Konner that the words we use to talk about soul and heart are critical, but that his own words are more descriptively accurate and more likely to sustain what Konner values.

We do not need to get into what Mary Midgley calls the "football match" view of discussions about human nature—those in which one perspective has to defeat the other and thereby win the day, even if our two authors might take this attitude.[7] A close look at some of Konner's passages show his own guardedness and qualifications. While the reader of his book might be impressed with the vastness and depth of the claims made for a scientific explanation, the motto he chose for his book, from Bertolt Brecht's *Life of Galileo*, is, "The aim of science is not to open the door to everlasting wisdom, but to set a limit on everlasting error" (xvi).

I have not counted the use of the word *only* as a claim for the importance of the views espoused, but my strong impression is that the theologian uses it far more frequently than the anthropologist. Also, toward the end of his book, Konner precedes his final quotation of his motto by saying, "It seems to me that so far we have applied our intelligence, and only our intelligence in ordering of human life on earth. It's not that I don't believe in the sheer power of intelligence. . . . It's that everywhere I turn in the world of science and scholarship I encounter people who believe in it much more than I do; people who serve it as if it were a god" (422). He goes on to cite Pope's *Essay on Man* to accent the importance of doubt; we should deem ourselves to be neither a god nor simply a beast (423). He is very close to Niebuhr's idea of man as "a curious compound of 'nature' and 'spirit.'"

Our two authors, different as they are, seem to be within speaking distance of each other. If they are, they have come there from very different starting points, from opposite directions. Niebuhr, like Heschel, starts from what is distinctively or uniquely human, in his view of things. Konner, like Wilson, starts from what we humans share with all of animal life, or even all of biological life. If it does not distort our understanding by assuming that "top" is more valued than "bottom," we can say that the theologian starts from the "top" and the bioanthropologist from the "bottom." I might put the contrast another way: Niebuhr emphasizes "spirit"; it is the central descriptive feature of the human. Konner emphasizes "nature"; the human cannot be properly understood without grounding an interpretation in biology. To establish this comparison I briefly analyze each account of the human.

We turn first to our theologian. Niebuhr's opening line, previously quoted, is memorable: "Man has always been his most vexing problem" (1:1). Description and explanation run together in his account of the human. One must remember that he insists that man "is a curious compound of 'nature' and 'spirit'" (1:viii). Support for this does not come from biology and biopsychology, but from his interpretation of the biblical traditions, which do not support a radical dualism of body and soul. In comparison with "Greek philosophy," the "Hebraic sense of the unity of body and soul is not destroyed while, on the other hand, spirit is conceived of as primarily a capacity for and affinity with the divine" (1:152). Niebuhr interprets the apostle Paul to support this.

However, the "essence" of the human, what I take to mean its distinguishing or unique characteristic, is "freedom" (1:17). Niebuhr writes, "His essence is free self-determination" (1:16). One seldom finds the word *freedom* in Konner's account; it is safe to assume that he consciously omits it. Niebuhr certainly recognizes our biological nature, that which Konner elucidates in detail. He notes that we have difficulty bringing our various impulses into harmony, but believes this is "not caused by the recalcitrance of

nature but occasioned by the freedom of the spirit" (1:40).
For Konner the ground of such disharmony is in our biological nature.

Niebuhr uses at least dialectical, and sometimes
paradoxical, statements about the human. The human condition is both "bound" and "free"; we have the capacity for
free self-determination but also are bound by our finite-
ness—our bodily and social and historical conditions. We
are, to cite one example of a paradox, "both limited and
limitless." Konner clearly rejects the latter. The paradox,
this doubleness in which all humans are involved brings
with it "anxiety" as its "inevitable concomitant." To be
human is to be free, writes Niebuhr, to be free is to be anx-
ious, and this anxiety is "the internal precondition of sin"
(1:182). We relieve our anxiety not by faith in the ultimate
goodness of God, a faith that always points to an ultimate
fulfillment beyond tragedy, but by seeking security through
pride: in our intellect, in our moral qualities, in our social
communities, and almost anything that can function as a
god. Or we seek to relieve our anxiety by lapsing into our
finitude, by denying our capacity for self-determination
and following our impulses or acquiescing in the conditions of life in which we find ourselves, and thus in sloth.

This sketch indicates what I mean by Niebuhr's approach to the human from the "top." The essential aspect of
the human is spirit; it is freedom. But our spirit, our freedom, is bound to bodily and historical conditions in that curious compound of human nature.

Both of these authors are wary of what human activity
can do to deface and even destroy much that is valued in
human life. For Niebuhr, our theologian, the source of this
is the temptation that leads us inevitably to sin, all those actions and relations in which we engage to overcome our
anxiety or insecurity by our own human power—both individual and collective power—all those things we do to establish our independence and sense of self-mastery, or

human mastery collectively (1:174). The evidence for sin, however, comes not only from biblical texts and interpretations, but also from observations and interpretations of human activity, or human experience.

Niebuhr's first series of Gifford Lectures in Edinburgh was given in the autumn of 1939 during the opening days and weeks of the war in Europe. Underneath or behind all the political, military, and economic events that led to that event, was, in Niebuhr's thinking, sin—the actions of collective pride, the use of power for a human mastery of history and of peoples, the failure to acknowledge a divine and eternal reality in light of which all human actions stand judged.

Note the importance of a descriptive and explanatory account of human nature here, and how that account can support an interpretation of events and courses of action that should follow from that interpretation. Niebuhr draws upon the resources of the Christian tradition, but the aim of that retrieval is not to argue for the orthodoxy of religious doctrines, or for a virtually magical authority of a special divine revelation. The truth of this description, informed as it is by biblical and Christian "myths," is finally verified in experience: "Common human experience can validate" the truth of what is biblically and theologically based (1:143). When Niebuhr writes about conscience he makes the general point quite clear; he argues that "a universal human experience, the sense of being commanded, placed under obligation and judged" requires presuppositions of the biblical faith. But that faith, once accepted, allows insight into and understanding of human experience that makes for deeper and more profound awareness. Indeed, he writes, that faith "illumines experience and is in turn validated by experience" (2:63).

Someone working from a more empirical tradition that looks for "data" to support a description and analysis of the human can respond to this claim. Does experience validate

Niebuhr's account? What evidence from experience is there in favor or against it? Have his moral and religious interests so impregnated his description that the morphology of his interpretation is tightly circular? Or is the general outcome of his evaluative description supportable from alternative standpoints, and with evidence from scientific studies of the human? If similarities exist between outcomes of various accounts with reference to how human beings ought to act in the visions of a better life in which there is greater harmony, is that because of some concurrence in descriptions? If the outcomes are dissimilar, is that because one view has false factual premises, inappropriate interpretive concepts, and inadequate theories? Which claims to "truth" or greater adequacy are now valid? Or are we faced with incommensurable claims because different fundamental perspectives are operative?

We cannot reduce our anthropologist's account of human nature to a brief description any more than our theologian's, but we must attempt to do so. Konner opens his "Prefatory Inquiry" with a few questions, already quoted, that have been asked for centuries: "Why we are what we are, why we do what we do, why we feel what we feel . . ." (xi). Note again the similarity to Niebuhr's opening sentence, "Man has always been his most vexing problem." Konner grandly attempts to fit relevant piecemeal explanations and observations into a coherent response to those inquiries. To do this he draws not only upon his own research, but also in an extraordinarily comprehensive way upon research from many pertinent fields including, as I noted, literary as well as scientific sources.

Part 2 of Konner's work, "Of Human Frailty," begs for far more summary than is possible in this chapter. In it he combines studies from genetics and biology on the one hand and environment and culture on the other to analyze rage, fear, joy, lust, love, grief, and gluttony. All through the book are explicit and implied critiques of accounts that avoid or do not fully use the biological accounts of human life and activity. At one point, drawing from the work of Ernst Mayr, Konner writes, "Biology chips away at the lofty human soul by, first, showing how easily its processes can be explained physiologically and, second, showing how much it shares, both in structure and in purpose, with the corresponding phenomena we see in other animals" (143). He argues, for example, against optimists who believe that proper cultural conditioning can eliminate violence—"It is subdued, reduced, dormant, yes. But it is never abolished. It is never nonexistent. It is always there" (206)—and challenges biologists who extrapolate from their research to optimistic visions of the future: "What ever happened to that school of thought according to which the pain of life was a part of the joy of life, or at least a place on the path to it? That belief that the embrace of, and triumph over difficulty, is more exhilarating than denial" (257)?

Konner has evidence and arguments to back his disdain for what he calls the "tinker theory" of human activity and experience: "According to the tinker theory, human behavior and experience are basically good and decent and healthy and warm and cooperative and intelligent, but something has gone a bit wrong somewhere" (414). Practitioners of this theory are economists, psychotherapists, and others. Konner reminds his readers that the classic tradition of tragic literature "is much more consonant with the biological view" (415). Its consistent "view of the dark side of human life," out of which the chorus cries that it is better to die than to live and best never to have been born at all, is more to the point than proposals from various sciences and professions to tinker with aspects of the human (415). The descriptions and their outcome begin to sound somewhat Niebuhrian!

In his chapter titled "Change," Konner stresses the limitations of human potential. With tongue in cheek, I think, he writes, "While we are waiting for human beings to be transformed by some combination of science and magic and the very best of will into the beautiful raw material we all want them to be," and then continues soberly, "we may lose our last chances to take actions of practical value that will ensure the people are around long enough for that ultimate transformation to come over them." In cold sobriety he concludes, "Recognizing the limitations of human nature, and the evil in it, is a necessary prerequisite to designing a social system that will minimize the effects of those limitations, the expression of that evil. That too, paradoxically, is a means of modification of human behavior" (406). If this does not come close enough to warrant pondering how different descriptions of the human can lead to similar outlooks, I add another quotation. After citing a novel about the Talmudic tradition of Polish Jews which stresses that man is evil from birth, Konner offers a paraphrase: "Human beings are irrevocably, biologically endowed with strong inclinations to feel and act in a manner that their own good judgment tells them to reprehend" (427). Sin, if I may use that term here, is not located in the human spirit with its freedom and anxiety, but in biologically endowed inclinations. One almost wants to say that it is "original," or that it is at least inevitable, though perhaps not necessary, to refer to another Niebuhrian comment.

Konner has nothing really good to say about religion, and certainly he is a naturalist in the sense that no transcendent reality is appealing to him, since he finds no evidence for it. He cannot ground his hope in a benevolent providence that promises fulfillment beyond tragedy, as Niebuhr can. His hope—for which little evidence is given and which seems slim even in the way in which it is introduced—is in the human. "Who knows what good may not yet lurk in the hearts of men? In the hope of discovering it, in the hope of bringing it forth to the light, in the hope that some mechanism of sublunary nurturance may yet cause it to thrive and grow, we may well set our heart and minds to a most momentous task." Then, "as a sort of amulet, a good-luck charm of tradition," he quotes a psalm and ends the chapter with "Amen. Selah" (420).

This sketch, bare as it is, illustrates what I mean by Konner's approach to the human from the "bottom." The essential aspect of the human is nature: human attitudes, outlooks, and behavior are powerfully directed, if not determined, by the biological natures we share with other animals and with the whole of living things. But this nature seems also to ground a sense of wonder—that experience also is real—and it seems not to rule out the sense of moral responsibility to which appeals can be made. Put too neatly we can say that for Konner the human is embodied in nature with capacities for something called spirit. For Niebuhr one can say that the human is spirit, curiously compounded with nature.

Konner's and Niebuhr's valuations of human life are somewhat similar, though they are certainly not the same. Their explanations of human life are radically different. These differences reflect various things. One is the intellectual and professional context or field from which each author comes. The disciplinary context or tradition from which come explanations of human life obviously affect what features of it are judged to be more decisive and often by extrapolation what is valued. Here one can illustrate beyond our two major authors. For example, Gary Becker's *The Economic Approach to Human Behavior* explains much of human behavior, including marriage and family, on the basis of maximizing individual utility in the market.[8] Other examples abound in biopsychology, sociology, and other fields. Different disciplines almost "naturally" isolate and emphasize different "causal" factors as the most critical in explaining, understanding, and interpreting human nature and action. Each assumes that its information, concepts, ideas, and forms of explanatory arguments are most adequate, or at least are necessary in a comprehensive account. Quite reasonably, if one wishes to recommend activities to govern or alter the course of human life, the discipline from which one comes focuses on what is judged to be the critical causal factor or factors. Valuations are correlated with explanations at least at one point: the crucial factors in explanation, valued not morally but for their explanatory powers, predispose any effort to make a normative valuation in their direction. This is a much more complex matter than can be developed in this chapter because what scholars value about human life is not just one factor—such as biological survival, economic well-being, or physical health—but many, and because multicausal analysis is necessarily adduced even when making the case for the greater importance of one kind of explanation.

The disciplinary contexts of our two principal authors predispose them to prefer different sources of "data" and concepts in their explanation and valuation of the human. To state it this way, however, makes their approaches sound accidental; each is also deeply persuaded that his approach bears the most truth, although truth has different connotations for each. Recall Niebuhr's sentence in the preface to the 1941 edition; he is persuaded that the Christian faith offers resources for understanding human nature that have been lost in modern culture. His main resources for truth-bearing ideas and insights are the Bible and selected figures in Christian theology. Those on which he draws are used often for their mythic qualities, that is, their capacities to disclose fundamentally real and presumably universal aspects of human life and action. Thus, in a sense, they heuristically disclose the realities of experience. We get to the circularity I indicated earlier, namely that faith illumines experience and is in turn validated by experience. Thus "experience" also becomes "data" disclosed by Christian myths and concepts, and the data validate their use. The Bible makes no hard claims for special supernatural revelation, nor for what we might call "empirical studies" of experience. The objective seems to be clear; the persuasiveness of the account is confirmed by its disclosive power as it issues in a deeper understanding of the human and guides human action. A further test is the moral outcome—in political, economic, and other effects—of the actions that it guides.

Konner, as I have indicated, wants a similar outcome of his work. But his data are drawn from the storehouse of many studies of the human by those who use basically scientific methods to develop them. Truthfulness for Konner is accordance of data with the biological realities of life, and the adequacy of theories to interpret that data. His case is strengthened, in his view, by the authority of the studies he adduces to support his complex and comprehensive account. But one misses something in Konner's work if one does not pay sufficient attention to the literary sources to which he refers. In this respect he is different from others who bear the mantle of modern sciences of the human— those who eschew other sources of understanding. And in the end Konner appeals to "the sense of wonder," something of human experience which, I think, he has not fully backed by the same kind of data he uses in his examination of rage, lust, love, etc.

"Experience," vaguely conceived, is a source for both our authors. Both, I think, claim that the outcome of their writings discloses something truthful about human life and action. The tests of the truth each seeks to convey differ. While both are basically coherent in the internal structures of their works, both, interestingly, make appeals that many readers would judge to be gaps in their arguments.

In Konner's case the gap is between the analytical account that sustains most of the book and the final chapter, "The Dawn of Wonder." The critical question is whether the previous analysis entails or necessitates that more poetic conclusion, whether it permits but does not necessitate it, or whether the conclusion contradicts the previous analysis. Has he tightly knit the previous analyses based on various sciences with the more poetic conclusion? Do the sciences provide an adequate explanation for the experience of wonder? Or is the source of evidence for that drawn from literary and poetic sources? I do not engage here in detailed argument to justify my answer to this issue; I think that Konner's last chapter is not necessitated by the previous analysis, nor does it fully contradict what comes before. It is permitted and makes sense only if an aspect of human experience not fully explained in the previous materials is adduced. That aspect is "spirit," but not in Niebuhr's sense of freedom. While it opens a door to hope, it also cannot guarantee a final outcome "beyond tragedy."

Niebuhr does have confidence in a final outcome beyond tragedy, and the hope that this ensures is critical to his interpretation of the human prospect, as is his confidence in the reality of the mercy of God to forgive our failures and errors. These two appeals to faith provide the conditions, necessary conditions for Niebuhr, to live and act in the morass of moral and political ambiguity—ambiguity that Konner affirms in his own way. The basis for this mercy and hope comes with the Christian message, and Niebuhr is not loathe to use the word *only* with reference to that. If there is a gap between Konner's last chapter and the rest of his work, there is also a gap in Niebuhr's work. What each most appeals to for the sake of human well-being goes beyond the "data" each adduces from human life itself.

What is at stake between an avowedly theological and an avowedly scientific account of the human? It is not appropriate to generalize on the basis of our two introductory and our two principal authors. Konner and Wilson both consciously go beyond a purely scientific account to express a way of viewing the world. Both, I think, are hopeful in the long run that the sciences will provide exhaustive explanations of mental activity, human intentionality, and action—all matters that Niebuhr packs into his views of spirit and freedom and Heschel into his idea of responsive-ness. Each of their accounts is subject to assessment of its use of the various sciences or on purely scientific grounds, a matter I am not competent to undertake. But both Konner and Wilson are moralists in a nonpejorative sense; both have a message to bring to the world in the hope that it will be heard and will guide action so as to avoid further evils.

Niebuhr and Heschel do not represent "theology" as a whole. Heschel does not represent orthodox Judaism, espe-cially in its Talmudic or legal form. And Niebuhr, as I noted, is not a defender of creedal orthodoxy in Christianity, in-cluding the conviction of more orthodox thinkers that the Christian message is authorized by an exclusive special rev-elation, though he clearly finds that it discloses (reveals) the depths of the human predicament and provides assurance of forgiveness and a hope beyond tragedy. (His frequent use of the word *only* does, however, support a more theologi-cally conservative interpretation than I have given his work.) Whether one would find more theological critics of Niebuhr and Heschel than one would find scientific critics of Konner and Wilson is an interesting matter I will not pursue. But both of the theologians also have a message to bring to the world in the hope that it will be heard and guide action so as to avoid further evils.

I confine my closing remarks to our principal authors. If the moral outcome, the expression of wisdom, were the *only* purpose of writings like Konner's and Niebuhr's, and if the outcomes are as similar as I propose theirs are, it would not make much difference what arguments were adduced. The beneficial pragmatic outcome would justify the differ-ent arguments each makes. I think, however, that neither of them first determined what attitude toward the world he wanted to support and then simply found evidence and ar-guments to back it. One does find writings that intend to ei-ther frighten or assure their readers. For example, Hans Jonas, in his *The Imperative of Responsibility*, deliberately uses what he calls the heuristics of fear, though the argument that backs the fear he evokes is well made. And one finds rather utopian extrapolations made from limited evidence to evoke hope on the part of readers; Joseph Fletcher's *The Ethics of Genetic Control: Ending Reproductive Roulette* is one example.[9]

Of course, each addresses a different readership. Most of Konner's readers would find Niebuhr's work to be esoteric, unintelligible, and, for its use of very Christian themes and symbols, even offensive. At least many of Niebuhr's readers would find Konner's work to require some mastery of scientific materials they have only read about in news weeklies or seen portrayed on television, and would likely believe him to be reductionistic in his confidence in science. Perhaps some who have imbibed certain forms of critical theory would call science the myth of the twentieth century in that it provides the symbols for understanding reality; so it is the use of one reality disclosing myth against another. Some critics of each work might accuse the authors of intellectual arrogance, a charge that requires qualification by careful reading of each. To radically polarize these books, however, is to take Midgley's football-match view of intellectual discourse—one in which one side must defeat the other.

Even though both of our principal authors rhetorically move to an impact on the reader's view of life in the world, they are concerned for the "truthfulness" of the evidence adduced to support it. Of course, every author makes such a claim. But Niebuhr's appeal to experience is different from that of many other religious writers; it also is not "data" in the sense that Konner's material is. And Konner's "data" refer to the biological basis of "experience." This is what makes it interesting to focus on these works.

Have we come to the old issue of "two cultures," the humanities and the sciences, once again? In a sense we have, but the overlap of outcomes makes it possible to move beyond a confrontational relation between the two. Special attention must be given to the importance of literary sources for Konner; as previously noted, the motto of his book comes not from a biologist but from Bertolt Brecht. His use of literary sources discloses meaning and wider significance—a kind of truthfulness comes from the creative writer whose reflections are not backed by hard data. If this is the case in general, one can argue that symbols and concepts from religious traditions can (not necessarily do) also disclose significance or meaning. For Konner, I believe, the literary sources provide insight into meanings that cannot be reduced to the scientific explanations that provide the main basis of his argument. But they also do not stand over against that material; they add to and disclose wider significance of it in the light of Konner's profound concern for human well-being.

Much of the research used by Konner has been developed since Niebuhr wrote his book, and in his later writings Niebuhr was quite receptive to sources drawn particularly from Erik Erikson's work. It can be argued that a theologian's account, insofar as it seeks to describe and explain human experience can, and ought to, be open to the empirical sciences such as Konner's work portrays. This need not be any less uncritical than Konner himself is, for example, in his critiques of what he calls the "tinker theory," but it can help to make a theological account intelligible to a nonreligious public, and it can provide other evidence, less intuitive, to support the theologian's positions. The theologian's concern for the well-being of life can be backed by and, in its details, informed and *corrected by* such works as Konner's. They might function to shed distinctive light, like that coming from Brecht and others.

Truthfulness about the human situation can be found in both scientific and religious sources—as well as other literary ones. An exchange between theology and the human sciences need not be a polarized confrontation. But this

prudent generosity can mask critical issues in particular investigations where the sources are, to all appearances at
least, in conflict. How traffic from different disciplines and
outlooks intersects at the human is illumined by analyzing
a meeting of theology and bioanthropology. Further analysis of the intersections of biology and medicine with ethics
and theology follows in the next four chapters.

2 Moral Discourse about Medicine: A Variety of Forms

Introduction

What are the boundaries of medical ethics? Who decides them? What do health professions conceive the focus of medical ethics to be: clinical choices, research issues, health care distribution policies? Perhaps the more interesting question is, What are medical ethics not? Can sharp boundaries be defined between medical ethics and medical economics or sociology? Is the decision process in the United States Congress and the National Institutes of Health what determines which diseases receive priority in biomedical research funding medical ethics, or medical politics? Are comparative studies of the justice of health care delivery systems between the United Kingdom, Sweden, and the United States studies in medical ethics, or studies in medical economics and politics?

Who has the authority to define the technical parameters and perimeters of medical ethics? Is it the various participants in medical practice and policy formation, or is it philosophers and theologians with their admirable penchant for conceptual clarity and precise distinctions? Does a sense that something is wrong with the distribution of biomedical research funding, the accessibility of health care, the "medicalization" of society count as a moral concern? Or is such an uneasiness so inchoate or so conceptually muddled that it can be ignored by scholars in medical ethics? Or do the concepts and procedures of moral philosophy or moral theology define the ethical?

If clinical and research moral quandaries make up the focus of medical ethics, can they be adequately grasped, understood, and explained without accounting for the sociology of research, of health care delivery systems, and of hierarchies of prestige and power in hospitals? Can they be understood and explained without taking into account medical economics and medical politics, or changing cultural and personal values, individual aspirations and goals, and other elements of contemporary ethos?

What happens to the scope of medical ethics when the high drama of extreme cases becomes the focus of attention? What happens when court cases become prominent if not dominant data in ethics courses and articles? What happens when moral philosophers and theologians, like so many psychiatrists, can be lined up to offer testimony for both the prosecution and the defense?

These questions come from the digging and spading, the ruminations, of one who has never been at the center of the field of medical ethics, but who has been in and out of it since about 1961, before medical ethics became a growth industry. This chapter is not based upon comprehensive study of the large body of medical ethics literature, but upon broad though selective reading. Its title uses the term "moral discourse" precisely to espouse inclusion of a variety of literature. "Morally relevant discourse" might be even more appropriate, and certainly would be to any who desire to keep strict and technical limits to the language of ethics and its concepts and procedures of argumentation. It does not take on the old problem of sharply distinguishing between the moral, the nonmoral, and the premoral, but it appeals to a generosity on the part of readers to tolerate some ambiguity for the sake of clarity on a different level.

In literature about medicine, as well as literature about economics, politics, and other activities, four types of moral discourse are distinguishable. I shall call these ethical, prophetic, narrative, and policy discourse. The argument of this chapter is that if too exclusive attention is given to any one of the types, significant issues of concern to morally sensitive persons and communities are left unattended. My suggestion is that none of the types is sufficient in itself. The contributions of each type to the other and to a larger framework of medical moral literature is not fully developed there.

The four types have in common a concern for various human values; each is prompted, in my judgment, by an uneasiness, a sense that something is awry. And each sees a different location for what is perceived to be inadequate if not wrong, and thus uses language or forms of discourse appropriate to that location. Each uses the data, information, sources of insight, and concepts that are judged to be appropriate to the location or arena in which some wrong is intuited or perceived.

Ethical Discourse

The center of ethical discourse, as I use the term, is the use of concepts, distinctions, and modes of discourse formulated over centuries in the disciplines of moral philosophy and moral theology. All readers of contemporary medical literature are familiar with the framing of problems and solutions by a relatively small set of concepts: rights, duties, obligations, competence, and justice. Also familiar are various allegedly helpful distinctions: between competent and noncompetent patients, between active and passive euthanasia, between reversible and irreversible medical conditions, between various probabilities of effective outcomes of interventions, and the like.

The modes of argumentation in ethical discourse are often known by the typological and occasionally useful distinctions of moral philosophers, such as deontological and utilitarian. The quandaries that provoke reflection are typically those of conflicts of rights and duties, of degrees of acceptable risk, of allocation of scarce medical resources, of the moral status of patients—whether they have the capacities that mark them as persons, and so on. The procedure for examining these issues is often the classic one of casuistry, the application of principles to cases.

Cases are developed by professional medical persons using information derived from clinical tests and from the experience of clinicians; comparison to other cases is often used to sharpen the similarities and dissimilarities between cases. The prognoses of various courses of action, based upon medical science and clinical experience, are considered. Salient features are those that locate not only the medical but also the moral issue.

A procedure such as abortion can be addressed as a moral problem; within such a class of cases particular circumstances require a different degree of refinement of ethical analysis and choice. For example, the abortion issue is addressed as a very large class, and arguments for or against its morality address all possible occasions for the intervention. If, however, the procedure is not ruled out as immoral, more refined ethical analysis is required to judge the moral propriety of a specific abortion in relation to specific fetal conditions or conditions of the mother.

Similar concepts and procedures are used in other critical choices that currently occupy physicians, ethicists, lawyers, and the public, for example, the appropriateness of using artificial procedures of nutrition in noncognitive patients and, more controversially, of removing them once they have begun. The literature is replete with case studies; many people find them endlessly fascinating because most focus on choices about death and thus have a sense of high drama.

Arguments about classes of cases or about particular cases often reflect preferences for different theories of morality, whether the debaters are conscious of them or not. For example, arguments appealing to rights have a different focus from arguments appealing to probable outcomes and qualities of life.

My favorite illustration of the concept above comes from a discussion of proposed legislation, but the arguments reflect commitments to opposing views of the moral obligations of the medical professions. The legislation was the Uniform Anatomical Gifts Act; the discussants were colleagues in renal therapy. The surgeon at that time objected to the restriction the act placed on access to organs that could be used to save lives of other patients. The internist argued vehemently in favor of the act because it preserved the rights of the deceased and next of kin to determine the disposition of the corpse. The surgeon implicitly believed that the ethically sanctioned calling of the profession was to save the greatest number of lives possible, and thus the means to fulfill this vocation ought not be unduly restricted on moral and legal grounds. Clearly, the internist was defending a moral tradition that primarily honored the right of individuals, even though choices made might deprive other persons of potential benefits.

Different preferences for different ethical theories (or probably, in this case, preferences that were not for theories but for beliefs about morality) selected different aspects of the class of cases as the morally salient ones. In effect, the same information in each case received different degrees of moral valence as a result of different theories of morality.

The purpose of ethical discourse, as I use the term here, is to decide how one ought to act in particular circumstances. The concern typically is to find moral justification for a particular intervention or for nonintervention. This is the great and important contribution of ethical discourse. The circumscription around salient features is usually rather clearly drawn. The principal agent is clear: the responsible physician. The circumstances deemed to be morally relevant are limited, though arguments occur over these limits. The primary object of the action is unambiguous; it is the patient. The alternative means of action are stipulated by the medical profession; the intention is certainly always to seek the best interests of the patient. Probable outcomes can be judged on the basis of similar cases. And if there is no clear and fully logical reason for one choice or the other, at least certain options are closed out. The prudential judgment takes place within limits, and the act or the inaction is done with relative certitude of its morality. The risk of engaging in an unethical act is, if not eliminated, at least limited.[1]

Moral discourse, in this restricted sense of medical ethics, is obviously necessary, and its merits hardly need enumeration. The focus on particular acts and on a limited number of agents, however, requires assumptions that can be questioned from some other perspectives—perspectives that find other forms of moral discourse appropriate. There is not enough questioning of the propriety of high medical technology per se that is often the necessary condition for the existence of the quandaries that have to be resolved. The technology that is interposed between the patient and a "natural" time to die, for example, is not brought under critical judgment. Certain personal and cultural values are assumed, such as that the preservation of physical life under conditions of unusual adversity and limitation is an individual and social good. Only limited aspects of the patient's life story, his or her personal narrative, are taken into account; the relevant past tends to be brief.

For example, I once knew a young physician who was puzzled by an eighty-four-year-old patient's refusal of certain clinical tests. An older physician of Scandinavian origin asked a few questions and determined that the patient was an aged Scandinavian immigrant, and quietly said, "It is quite typical of a person his age from that culture to take a stoical attitude toward death." Also, the proper attitude of ethical discourse brackets emotions, affective responses, and physician's perceptions, which cannot be reduced to data and concepts appropriate to ethical discourse. The ethical, in the eyes of some, becomes its own technical fix, eliminating the importance of compassion and other moral sentiments. The social and economic structure of health care in the society is often assumed as a given, even if it is deemed less than what is desirable. For all these and other limitations of ethical discourse, however, it is necessary, but if moral discourse is excessively limited to it, medical morality becomes myopic.

Prophetic Discourse

One can say that prophetic discourse tends to be "macro" in comparison with ethical discourse, which tends to be "micro." Prophetic discourse is usually more general than ethical discourse and sometimes uses narratives to make prophetic points. It takes two distinguishable forms. One is indictment. Readers of the Bible know this from the writings of Hosea, Amos, and Jeremiah. The indictments are radical, that is, they are not occupied with surface issues but expose the roots of what is perceived to be fundamentally and systematically wrong. Prophets are seldom interested in specific acts except insofar as they signify a larger and deeper evil or danger. The discourse usually is passionate and often apocalyptic, and uses metaphors and analogies to stir the hearers' emotions. Evidence is marshaled to sustain the indictment, and while some prophetic voices take counterevidence into account and develop arguments, many do not. To the gloomy prophet much ethical discourse is simply rearranging the deck chairs on the Titanic when it is already sinking. Or developments appear to be on a course that is likely to lead to disaster if it is not halted. To the moral philosopher or theologian, the prophet's concerns often seem to be "global," the arguments poorly made, and the language too emotive.

The second form of prophetic discourse is utopian. The utopian prophet describes an alluring future in which ailments and maladies of persons and societies will be relieved and a healthier and happier condition realized. Utopian language, like the language of indictment, is often symbolic and metaphorical; it is visionary; it arouses human hopes; it raises human aspirations. To the policymaker the utopian prophet appears to be unrealistic, unwilling to face the limits of the present time, and lacking the patience to organize resources for the modest increments of improvement that can actually occur.

Ivan Illich's *Medical Nemesis* is announced by a paperback publisher in prophetic terms: "The most explosive, uncompromising . . . attack on the gravest health hazard we face today: our medical system."[2] Like many prophetic books it sharply divided those who found it deceptive in its use of evidence, unnuanced in its arguments, and fearmongering in its language, on the one hand, and those who were readily persuaded by its apocalyptic tone, on the other. Illich does not take up the kinds of clinical decisions that much of the literature of medical ethics addresses; he perceives underlying these and other problems a deeper evil, the system of modern medicine. Prophets frequently find a demonic or satanic reality that pervasively corrupts institutions and practices; Illich has his clearly in mind. And, like Hosea, Amos, and Cicero of old, Illich has a way with words, using similes, metaphors, analogies, and literary references that are charged with passion and create affective as much as (or more than) critical intellectual responses. A few examples from his chapter "The Medicalization of Life" suffice to illustrate this.

He opens a subsection of this chapter, "Political Transmission of Iatrogenic Disease," with a litany of events to show that medicine is now less concerned to enhance what occurs in nature and more concerned to "engineer the dreams of reason." The paragraph ends as follows: "But any charge against medicine for the clinical damage it causes constitutes only the first step in the indictment of pathogenic medicine. The trail beaten in the harvest is only a reminder of the greater damage done by the baron to the village his hunt overruns."[3]

One of the citations supporting the first of the quoted sentences is from a sociological article whose theme is that medicine is becoming a major institution of social control, either displacing or incorporating traditional institutions of religion and law, a place in which absolute judgments are being made by supposedly morally neutral and objective experts in the name of health. But note also the second quoted sentence, from which one infers that Illich's choice of language is meant to enhance a vision of innocent and powerless patients who are not fully aware of the greater damage being done by a powerful medical system of medical barons.

In another section, "Terminal Ceremonies," Illich begins his discussion in this way:

> Therapy reaches its apogee in the death-dance around the terminal patient. At a cost of between $500 and $2,000 per day, celebrants in white and blue envelop what remains of a patient in antiseptic smells. The more exotic the incense and the pyre, the more death mocks the priest. The religious use of medical technique has come to prevail over its technical purpose, and the line separating the physician from the mortician has been blurred.[4]

Other authors who are concerned about terminal procedures, their costs and their effects upon patients and others, describe the same set of conditions in less dramatic and affective language. Illich intends to affect the reader: procedures are death dances; physicians are priests in liturgical vestments; the scene is more exotic than a corpse on a pyre of sandalwood at the burning ghat in Benares; the role of the healer and burier can no longer be differentiated. The reader is presented with a redescription of events and conditions that allude to meanings of religious significance; an indictment of medicine is thereby implied if not explicit. It is not unlike the prophet Hosea's use of harlotry as a metaphor for religious negligence and disobedience among the people of Israel. Factual matters become charged with moral indignation through the similes and metaphors used.

Nor is it unlike a political speech by Cicero and countless politicians since his time. For example, in his speech against Catiline, Cicero spoke in these terms: "For imagine every type of criminality and wickedness you can think of: he has been behind them all. . . . Whenever all through these years there has been a murder, the murderer has been he. Not one single act of filthy lechery has been committed without him being its guiding spirit."[5] No medical ethical casuist uses this kind of language. But perhaps ethical discourse cannot readily indicate the systemic problems that Illich perceives, and it hardly arouses moral passions. Indeed, it deliberately seeks to bracket passions in favor of rationality.

Illich's is prophetic discourse in two important respects. He sees modern medicine to be at least as dangerous as it is beneficial and goes beneath the symptoms presented to isolate the major source of many ailments, namely the social system of modern medicine. The dominant evil, the devil, is named. Also he uses the rhetoric of advocacy, and the language is justified by its intended effect upon the reader. An indictment that might have been made in dry statistics and clearly developed linear argument is more forcefully made. One "feels" Illich's indignation, and he desires to arouse the reader's own.

Illich's prophetic address has value that ethical discourse does not achieve. Of course, the locations of the quandary are different. By locating problems systematically and socially, Illich at least calls attention to aspects of contemporary medicine that evoke uneasiness, and while his language is inflated from some perspectives, one is cognizant of aspects of modern medicine that might have escaped the attention of a morally conscientious clinician and a wider public. But Illich is hardly sufficient; his book does not aid the clinician in making a morally sound medical judgment, nor does it aid the policymakers in taking steps to improve medical research and care—steps that take one from where they are today to where they can and ought to be in a year's time.

Leon Kass would, no doubt, be appalled to see his work within the same class as Illich's. His prose is, except for an occasional flourish, undramatic; he is seldom given to hyperbole. His citations are less to current literature than to great classics of Western culture, and when a recent event is discussed it is used to point beneath itself to a deeper matter. He feels no need to bolster his articles with scores of citations to lend them authority as Illich does. He shows modesty about even his most dramatic forecasts, and is careful to modify any indictments with assurances that he appreciates the benefits of modern medicine and praises its accomplishments.

Nonetheless, the reader senses a profound moral passion, a deep concern for the effects of medical experimentation and high technological care on humane values that Kass obviously holds very dear. He is prophetic. He exposes apparent assumptions that seem not to be radically challenged by scientists and clinicians; he peers into the future to question potential outcomes of courses of events if the present routes continue. And he has a vision of what constitutes the good human life; though it is not argued for, it is averred. This vision is a kind of normative backdrop against which problematic aspects of modern science and medicine are exposed by his descriptions and analyses. His call is to a heightened consciousness so that the humanness that is to be valued is not eroded by incremental developments oblivious to their wider and deeper consequences.

What I mean by prophetic discourse can be illustrated from a number of Kass's essays. Medical ethics literature is replete with articles about in vitro fertilization, as is the legal literature. Kass approaches it differently. He writes, "The first task, it seems to me, is not to ask 'moral or immoral?' or 'right or wrong?' but to try to understand fully the meaning and significance of the proposed actions." For Kass "meaning and significance" refer to a much larger cultural and human context than does the ethicist's conventional question: "Is the procedure immoral?" or "Can it be ethically justified?" Meaning and significance for whom and for what? In Kass's analysis it is for all humanity. The foreseeable consequences and predictable extension of developing life in the laboratory touch "even our common acceptance of our own humanity." He writes, "At stake is the *idea* of the *humanness* of our human life and the meaning of our embodiment, our sexual being, and our relation to ancestors and descendants." In thinking about immediate decisions, the kinds of decisions ethical discourse deals with, Kass warns that "we must be mindful of the larger picture and must avoid the great danger of trivializing the matter for the sake of rendering it manageable."[6]

The larger picture is further developed in a paragraph that provides the backdrop against which his moral concerns about particular practices become highlighted.

> Our society is dangerously close to losing its grip on the meaning of some fundamental aspects of human existence. In reviewing the problem of the disrespect shown to embryonic and fetal life in our efforts to master them we noted a tendency . . . to reduce certain aspects of human being to mere body, a tendency opposed most decisively in the nearly universal prohibition of cannibalism.[7]

The use of cannibalism to make a point about what underlies in vitro fertilization, in his eyes, is a powerful prophetic insight; it is jarring. Kass goes on to discuss prohibitions against incest and adultery, which "defend the integrity of marriage, kinship, and especially the lines of origin and descent." He explains that "clarity about your origins is crucial for self-identity, itself important for self-respect." "It would be," he writes, "deplorable public policy to erode further such fundamental beliefs, values, institutions, and practices."[8]

In this discussion and in others, I maintain, Kass uses prophetic discourse. He peers through the immediate and confined things on which ethical discourse focuses to describe a more profound malady, one that is a threat to the whole of humanity. The things he values are stated; they are not argued for. And with a moral passion all the more eloquent because of its linguistic restraint, he can evoke a vision of a pending crisis.

My impression is that utopian prophetic discourse in medicine is rarer than it was some years ago. However, utopian outlooks seem to lie behind some of the inflated language that has been used to engage public support for certain research, such as announcing a "crusade" against cancer. Crusades have come to designate total war against an evil so great that any means of obliteration of the enemy is morally justifiable. A crusade provides support for more extreme measures than even a just war. The public also is titillated by the possibility of elimination of some death-dealing diseases, and evidence of radical containment, if not eradication, of smallpox and polio lend credence to other possibilities. Subtitles of books intimate utopian possibilities, for example, Joseph Fletcher, *The Ethics of Genetic Control: Ending Reproductive Roulette*, and Jose M. R. Delgado, *Physical Control of the Mind: Toward a Psychocivilized Society*. Perhaps without a utopian vision some investigators and social planners would lose incentive to work and alter social arrangements.

Delgado is not an unmitigated utopian; he is cognizant of pending moral and social problems from increased use of physical control of brain activity. But, to this reader, he cannot restrain some unguarded dreams.

> We are now on the verge of a process of mental liberation and self-domination which is a continuation of our evolution. Its experimental approach is based on the investigation of the depth of the brain in behaving subjects. Its practical applications do not rely on direct cerebral manipulations but on the integration of neuropsychological and psychological principles leading to a more intelligent education, starting from the moment of birth and continuing throughout life, with the preconceived plan of escaping from the blind focus of chance and of influencing cerebral mechanisms and mental structure in order to create a future man with greater personal freedom and originality, a member of a psychocivilized society, happier, less destructive, and better balanced than present man.[9]

A reader's response to such a statement in part depends on his or her own moral sensibilities and aspirations for the human future. One can infer an intention on the part of the author, however; he desires to move us by an alluring future of greater personal freedom and originality, of a happier, less destructive society. Readers might have a response that is the reverse of the intended; his is another vision that could justify research and application which could destroy social fabrics and human values as it is pursued.[10]

Alluring visions of a better medical and social future are clearly ambiguous, but their pursuit need not necessarily lead to blind neglect and destruction of existing values. Utopian prophets evoke hopes, and hope is a profound motivation for reducing the pain and suffering in the world.

Ethical discourse, because of the normal sharpness of its focus, does not stir the imagination to engage in larger medical pursuits; its normal language does not induce dreams. The issue is, of course, not only what evokes hope but what is the proper object of hope. My quotation from Delgado creates deep anxieties for persons who hold many values dear; it is also the case that a vision, perhaps judged to be utopian at one point in history—of a world without smallpox and polio, for example, or of an agriculture that can provide nutrients sufficient for all humankind—has issued in benefits.

Narrative Discourse

"Narrative ethics" are currently discussed and recommended by significant authors in religious ethical traditions, particularly Christianity. Oversimply, the principal line of argument is that we are members of moral communities, and the outlooks, values, and visions of these communities are shaped by their stories. As we participate in a community and its formative narratives, our own moral outlooks and values are shaped by its narrative. As such, this line of argument is descriptive, and its defense relies upon historical, sociological, and social-psychological evidence.

The critical issue, from a moral point of view, is what narratives ought to shape moral ethos and character. On certain theological grounds, it is argued that the Christian story ought to shape the Christian community and characters of Christian people, and even that the morality of Christians ought to be tested by its faithfulness to its own story.[11]

This larger thesis of narrative ethics is not the point of introducing it in this chapter, though one book I will cite provides a good example of medical education as a process of internalization (and some resistance to it) that takes place as students are shaped by the "narrative," broadly conceived, of the medical profession.

Narratives are not arguments in the sense that ethical discourse provides arguments. However, one must note the extent to which storytelling (using various cases and experiences) occurs when clinical moral choices are discussed. At such a juncture the story functions similarly to parables in biblical and rabbinic literature; one asks a question of a wise person and hears a story that does not really prescribe precise conduct but illumines one's choice. The moral philosopher or theologian is often frustrated by the use of narrative; its logic is not that of moral arguments as normally conceived. The philosopher may abstract from the narrative an implied argument which might or might not be persuasive on his or her grounds. But the teller of the story would believe that important affective and descriptive overtones are thus dissolved by the abstraction.

Narratives can provide a more extended context within which the circumstances of a particular clinical choice are understood or in which a medical policy is proposed. Whether and how that larger understanding should be taken into account in a particular choice is a matter of dispute. A chapter by Renée Fox and Judith Swazey, "The Case of the Artificial Heart," provides an example worthy of reflection. From one perspective it is a study in medical sociology, medical history, or even medical politics, but not in medical ethics.

The central narrative follows the case of Haskell Karp, who received the first implanted mechanical heart. Around it is an interpretive report of an unfolding sequence of events that gives details about the competition between Drs. DeBakey and Cooley, along with other relevant aspects. Research has been done in primary documents, interviews conducted, and so on. The chapter is not ethical discourse; it does not provide the kinds of arguments that scores of other articles on artificial hearts have done. At the end of a fascinating and informative account, the authors close with a modest conclusion: "In our view, this case and its outcome show that the medical and law professions, and the larger society to which they belong, have not satisfactorily dealt with the social, moral and legal issues involved in therapeutic innovation with human subjects."[12]

The technical medical ethicist could agree with that, and might press the authors for specific formulations of rules or guidelines to govern future events. But that would miss the point. Because of historical, sociological, economic, and other aspects of their account, the authors force the reflective reader into a much larger context of discussion that Fox and others have called medical morality rather than medical ethics. Structures of institutions, sources of funding, competitiveness among investigators, motivations of desperate patients and their families, technological developments—these and other features frame specific moral medical choices. To separate the precise clinical choice from the more extensive factors leads to only partial understanding, if not gross misunderstanding, of the problem to be addressed. The authors' account points to many junctures in which critical choices are made, and the adequate moral response requires attention to the proper ends and means for each of them. Whether this wider context would make a difference in the clinical choice itself is not as clear.

Melvin Konner's narrative interpretation of his experience as a medical student after a decade of teaching and publication in anthropology is also morally significant. *Becoming a Doctor: A Journey of Initiation in Medical School* is the story of becoming socialized into a profession by participating in its "narrative," and of Konner's resisting aspects of the resulting formation of professional character.[13] He not only portrays his own experience, but also records his apt perceptions of institutional arrangements, characteristics of various physicians and their conduct, the effects of strenuous pressures on young doctors, and many other things. His response is that of a mature and deeply humane student confronting the impersonal and objectified circumstances of a modern teaching hospital, and the effects of these circumstances on some patients.

Konner's is not a diatribe against the dehumanization of modern medical care in such institutions; he does not argue from a theory of justice to portray injustices in health care; it is not a theory-laden book, not even theory from Konner's own discipline of anthropology. Its impact on the reader is all the greater because of that. The narrative portrays an ethos, a pervasive climate in large urban teaching hospitals; it has a prophetic impact. There is no theory about how the ethos is internalized in the becoming physician, though an anthropologist certainly would have one. There is no theory of "ethos" itself. But the reader feels the impact of the ethos on the development of the professional character of physicians. While Konner has his heroes, such as Dr. Ringler, who sustain outlooks, concerns, and relations that are commendable, he does not explain how such persons have come to have and sustain commendable qualities against some odds. One gets a sense that by showing good qualities one knows them; there is no argument about why they are good.

Narratives like this stay close to experience, which is precisely their great merit. The term *ethics* tends to abstract from experience; this is its merit. But both are important forms of moral discourse. The author of a narrative, in ways comparable to prophetic authors, can ask of the moral philosopher: What is the context in which choices are made? What are underlying social practices and assumptions, the accepted conditions, the institutional arrangements, and the human emotions involved? Do they have to be addressed morally as much as the clinical case has to be? But none of the forms of discourse I have isolated is self-sufficient; they often overlap and supplement each other.

Policy Discourse

Literature on various aspects of medical policy is profuse. Some of it is descriptive, such as studies of the politics of

biomedical research funding. Some of it is multidiscipli-
nary, such as the reports of presidential commissions on
various aspects of research and care. Some of it is ethical,
such as distributive justice concepts framing alternative
possibilities for health care distribution.

In this chapter I can only suggest a comparison between
the approach to policy from a very disciplined use of ethical
discourse and a hypothetical approach from the standpoint
of persons who have institutional roles that require them to
formulate policy within the limitations and possibilities of
resources accessible to them. Gene Outka's oft-reprinted
article on equal access to health care, "Social Justice and
Equal Access to Health Care," serves as my example of a rigorous approach.[14] It assumes a societal goal of assurance of
adequate health care to all persons in the nation. In the development of his argument to justify the goal, Outka delin-
eates the classic and standard concepts of distributive justice; similar cases should be treated similarly, but what
constitutes relevant similarity? Need? Ability to pay? Social
merit? He assesses the relevance of each of these concep-
tions and suggests institutional implications of his own
conclusion. The great merit of this article is precisely that
ethical discourse is dominant; it frames the analysis and
proceeds with rigor and precision to disclose implications of
various views of justice.

The contrast I wish to suggest is with an approach to
the same subject in which the language and information of
economics, politics, sociology, and medicine would be dominant. Outka's article represents, properly, the standpoint of
the ethical observer, an outsider to the institutions and
roles through which choices have outcomes. His primary
question is: What ought to be the case? Contrariwise, from
the standpoint of various engaged agents (who are more
likely to use the language of economics, politics, sociology,
and medical technology), the first questions are usually:
What is possible?[15] What resources are available or can be

accumulated? What proper interests compete for these resources? What personnel and institutional arrangements are necessary? If it is not the prior question, the question of what is possible is asked at least in tandem with questions more distinctively ethical. Information, relevant concepts, interpersonal sensitivities, relations to other institutions, and other factors all have to be on the table for analysis. The "ought" questions are answered within possibilities and limitations of what resources exist or can be accumulated and organized.

Policy discourse, from the perspective of agents responsible for resource allocations cannot be purely ethical. Enabling and limiting conditions ground possible courses of action. As theologians are wont to say, the good is sought under the conditions of finitude. Actually policy is seldom, if ever, determined by the conclusion of a formal ethical argument. But this does not eliminate the importance of the ethical analysis and argument; such argument articulates ends, refines the criteria for the moral choices embedded in the empirical, and facilitates moral self-evaluation. Policy discourse without ethical discourse easily degenerates into satisfaction with the merely possible, with assumed values and procedures, with the domination of the economic or institutional considerations. If ethical discourse can become encapsulated in its own concepts and modes of argumentation, so also can policy discourse, unless it is subjected to the ethical discourse.

Prophetic discourse, such as Illich's, often looks global and unrealistic to the policymaker, but its perspective can function to jar institutions from blind acceptance of the status quo. Narrative can inform the policymaker of the larger and more inclusive "story" for which they are developing a subplot, but it is not decisive in determining what ought to be done. For example, board members and administrators of health systems do well to read Paul Starr's historical and sociological account of medicine in the United

States, *The Social Transformation of American Medicine*, to grasp what has brought them to their present circumstances.

Conclusion

To focus moral discourse about medicine too exclusively on what I have described as ethical tends to lose sight of realms of choice and activity that are of great importance. Ethical discourse is not sufficient. But neither is prophetic, narrative, or policy discourse. The location of choices, of the perceived moral uneasiness or possibilities, licenses each of the forms of discourse described. Perhaps, though it is not argued here, the location of the uneasiness should determine the concept, approaches, language, and information that are appropriate, rather than a form of discourse determining what is and is not taken into account as morally relevant. At least there are different "moments" in medical morality when different forms are more appropriate. The contributions of each to the others in moral reflection about medicine is a topic for further investigation. This chapter has not focused on theological ethical literature about medical ethics. Chapter 3 develops a typology of these strategies for directing traffic in that intersection.

3 Styles of Religious Reflection in Medical Ethics

ary Midgley writes, "The main dispute in ethics these days lies between people who stress the *autonomy* of morals to avoid debasing them, and those who stress the *continuity of morals with other topics* in order to make them intelligible."[1] This is the text I elaborate on, respond to, and apply in this chapter.

Three alternative strategies of religious medical ethics are developed in this chapter. First, there is a literature in Christian and other religious ethics, whether applied to medicine or other human activity, which assumes and defends the "autonomy" of religious ethics. This autonomy is justified on the basis of biblical authority, the authority of tradition, or the authority of religious institutions. Autonomous religious ethics then are applied to medicine.

Second, there is a literature in Christian and other religious ethics, whether applied to medicine or other human activity, which interprets morals in continuity with other topics, such as natural appetites and the human condition, in order to make ethics intelligible both within the religious community and beyond it. Religious ethics are described and explained, and their application to medicine is interpreted.

Third, there is religious literature in which the explanation and interpretation of morals and the justification of ethics interact in a dialectical way, which leads to proposed changes in religious thought.

This is an ideal-typology. An ideal-typology is not a taxonomic device, into which various authors can be slotted, but a construct which, if it has value, has heuristic value. A type, when properly used, illumines the particularities of positions that in a general way fit it; it shows the particularities of positions as illumined by the type. Some literature can be interpreted in light of all three types.

Autonomy

Authors who assume the autonomy of religious ethics are deeply concerned to maintain the integrity, identity, and particularity of a religious and theological position. This type can be defended in various ways, but it always makes a case for the distinctiveness, the specificity or singularity, or the uniqueness of the religious position—its authorization as a way of interpreting life in the world, its vision of the ends to be achieved, its standards of human conduct, and the depth of commitment it requires.

One defense, currently supported by a general movement in intellectual and academic life, is what used to be called the sociology of knowledge. All constructions of reality, as a whole or in particular aspects, are related to points of departure that have particular social, cultural, political, economic, or ideological bases. The playing field of disciplines, if not level, is more level than many proponents of universal objectivity believed about what is known. A line of critical inquiry, which historically had many of its origins in the history of modern theology, now pervades efforts to deal with everything from mathematics and physics to literature, religion, and morality.

In its most radical forms, what used to be called presupposition hunting (something some theologians were quite skilled at doing with reference to other fields of inquiry) leads to the cacophony of intellectual and academic discourse, to not only relationalism but also extreme cognitive relativism. If this relativism is the case for the study of politics and nature, their claims for truth are no more secure than the claims made by a historic religious community, Christian, Jewish, Islamic, Buddhist, or any other. Thus, in this cacophony of voices, it is legitimate for representatives of Christian and other perspectives and traditions to define their particularity, and to join the noisy chorus in an effort to be heard. They have as much right as do rationalist moral philosophers since the latter also are tradition related, if not bound; all are partial and ideological.

Of course, debates continue about ethics not only among philosophers, but also within religious communities: which is the authentic representation of particularity, for example, Christian ethics, to be affirmed? Within a more general "postmodern" justification of a religious ethics, and there its right and responsibility to speak distinctively, arguments still occur as to which account of religious ethics is correct, or can best be defended. No one, to my knowledge, is willing to acquiesce to the judgment that any interpretation of ethics than can be denominated Christian or Jewish is equally plausible or valid. My point is simple; there is a license for religious ethics to be particular, since all positions are relative; yet one delineation of that particularity is judged to be correct and others wrong, or at least one is better than others. Is the distinctiveness to be found in the rules of action, or action guides; or is it to be found in the interiority, the ultimate intentionality of the agents? Is it to be found in the characteristics that shape the persistent patterns of outlooks and actions of the religious persons or communities, or is it to be found in the interpretations of the direction of the historical or even the cosmic process?

"Postmodernism" makes persons acutely aware of their particularities, and this has been accepted as an inevitability of thinking and acting. So, religious outlooks on medical and other activities are context related if not determined. This being the case, partiality is justified and affirmed, rather than being viewed as something to be constrained if not overcome. The arguments in favor of accepting relativism, per se, do not resolve disputes about whether it is essential to an accurate account of Christian ethics, for example. So criteria of evaluation are used to defend one interpretation as more authentic than others.

A second defense of the autonomy of religious ethics is based on a strong doctrine of particular revelation, whether to and through Moses, Jesus, or Muhammad. This defense is stated boldly and flatly in evangelical fundamentalist ethics on issues of homosexuality and abortion, and more subtly and in mediated forms in other Christian movements (and other religious traditions). The general point is held by all traditionally orthodox theologies that belong to what have been called Abrahamic religions and ethics: God chose to be revealed to, in, and through particular persons or events that are narrated, reflected upon, and authorized in sacred texts.

This defense can be contrasted to the first. Revealed truth, not historical relativity, is claimed as the basis of distinctive particularity, and thus the autonomy of theology and religious ethics. Because of this truth, the community and its ethical writers are bound faithfully to interpret the sacred texts.

Sometimes this leads to a specifically revealed morality, as in the Decalogue, and maybe in the application of the covenant and other biblical codes of morality and holiness. Christians make a distinction between the authority of the moral codes and the ritual or cultic codes in the Bible. This implies either that some ethical criteria make the moral codes more authentic revelation than the cultic codes (see

Aquinas, Calvin, Hooker, and many others), or that God intended the cultic to have a historical sunset clause but did not intend such for the moral. The development of such a revealed morality differs among religious traditions and certainly within them.

The procedures of halakic reasoning in the Orthodox Jewish tradition are intellectually complex. A biblical text is examined for its biblical applications and their relations to other biblical contexts, developing a tradition of interpretations that also is taken into account. Later codified forms and the interpretations of particular rabbis ascend to higher authority, so the work of a judge, or decisor, on a current medical matter is grounded in divine revelation, and in knowledge of the interpretation of the tradition through a distinctive casuistical process. A life of holiness is fulfilled by conformity to the law; one is brought into the presence of God by obedience. Some Christians, in contrast, isolate a biblical judgment and apply it directly to some current proposed procedure.

The distinctive center of revelation within sacred texts makes a difference in the revealed theological backing of medical and other ethics. For example, Barth's Christocentric theology leads to both different ethical procedures and to some different judgments from classic Thomistic or Lutheran ones. If the revelation centers on historical liberation one has a different basis for ethics from revelation being centered on the cross, or on the mercy and forgiveness of God. The cosmic significance of Christ and the consequent *theosis* in Eastern Orthodoxy lead to different ethics from those based on the conviction that the life of the one in and through whom God is revealed is the normative shape and pattern of moral fidelity. These differences, while all claiming a basis in revelation, can and do affect the norms and procedures of medical ethics.

In some forms of Christian, Jewish, and Islamic ethics, revelation in the sacred text is developed through authorized strands of tradition, though arguments exist about the correct interpretation and elaboration. Tradition authorizes certain approaches to medical ethics; some particular moral precepts are judged in some instances to be unexceptionable. The continuity of reflection through centuries creates a presumption of moral correctness; the weight of the argument is in favor of tradition. Dissent has to mount argument from defensive positions. But tradition is not static. Development in tradition can be historically demonstrated in many cases, as scholars have done in studies of war, usury, contraception, and other issues.

What backs the authority of tradition in religious medical ethics? One factor is the conviction that the distillation of ends and rules is the outcome of the thinking of those who are wise—always men until very recently. History seems to sift out what is judged to be wisdom from what is judged to be folly. Special authority accrues around persons and writings that have articulated procedures of thinking and moral ideas and ideals that are sustained by subsequent generations.

A second support is communal practice, and not just ideas. Certain practices achieve the status of authenticity through time because they reflect fidelity to the revelation and apparently issue in activities and ends that are morally appropriate to the faith and beliefs. This may be supported theologically in Christianity by a view that the Spirit works through the thought and practices of both the leaders and members of the community, guiding them faithfully through different courses of events and different circumstances. The autonomy of religious ethics is backed by the authority of tradition, which is shaped by consensus of the faithful.

Institutional authority provides a third support for the autonomy of religious ethics. Structures of power develop that authorize certain persons to speak for the revealed and traditional authorities. Means develop for the faithful to assess the degree of their compliance, and to have that compliance or noncompliance judged by empowered persons or communities. Authentic interpretation and application of revelation and tradition is sometimes controlled by persons in offices. If their power to allure consent and obedience is not sufficient, there are institutional means for enforcement and prescribed actions for bringing the wayward back into good standing. Or, in less formally authorized structures of power, more subtle forms function to gain consent and compliance, such as shunning or banning. The autonomy of religious ethics is backed by the autonomy of religious institutions. The institutional guardians of the revelation and tradition, even when the tradition has been shaped by many nonbiblical sources, uphold and speak for the distinctiveness, specificity, singularity, or uniqueness, or at least for the integrity and autonomy of a religious ethics.

I have not shown how these types illumine medical ethics, and how they are modified in their application. The basic ideal-construct is clear: religious ethics are autonomous, at least in the sense that they have an authorization that is specific to them. They are applied to medical matters; the traffic across the intersection to medical matters is basically in one direction. Alteration of religious ethics by the findings of science, medicine, and other disciplines is resisted. This helps us to understand the medical ethical writings of many important Protestants and Catholics, and those of important writers in the Jewish and Islamic traditions as well. Distinctiveness is affirmed in some way; some independence is claimed; and there is deep concern to show how faithfulness to that authorization directs human conduct in medical matters. Distinctiveness is not only practiced; it is also justified.

Continuity

Now to the second point in my text from Midgley. There is a literature in Christian and other religious ethics pertaining to medicine and other areas of activity that interprets morality in continuity with other topics to make religious ethics intelligible within and beyond the religious communities. Morality and ethics are explained; how they can be Christian or Jewish, or in some broad sense religious, is described. Thus religious ethics (or religious medical ethics) become intelligible, and therefore understandable, tolerable, or even persuasive, especially if they add increments of depth or scope to what other views ignore or do not address sufficiently.

Here Midgley adds that some scholars stress the continuity of morals with other topics. I show how intelligibility is gained by demonstrating continuity between religious ethics and other ethics. Religious ethics belong to the class of ethics; religions (Christianity and others) qualify ethics to make them a subclass. A few illustrations of this point follow.

A specific literature exists to describe how rules govern, or at least direct, decision making in many spheres of human activity and experience: economic, familial, political, legal, etc. There are all sorts of rules; to be governed or directed by rules is common in human experience. Morality shares with other areas of experience and activity the phenomenon of rules. But moral life is different from other arenas of rule-governed activity, or at least distinctive in its dimensions. Rules can be moral in character, rather than legal or bureaucratic, or can govern social roles. Some position has to be taken on what distinguishes moral rules from other rules, and on that point there is no consensus. I will not expound here on that subissue, except to say that morality is continuous with other "topics" in that it deals with a system of rules that govern behavior; to make this point makes morality intelligible in a certain context.

Religious morality, according to some views, is also a morality of rules. Historical evidence for this can be found in historic religious traditions that have developed moral rules and moral codes. Some of these become legal in form because sanctions can be used against violators, or because the procedures involved in their application are similar to procedures involved in different legal traditions. A rule, or a command, such as the command to love one's neighbor as oneself, is an example. Others are more specific in the actions they prescribe or proscribe. Thus, religious morality or religious ethics are continuous with ethics interpreted as rules.

What makes a rule of religious morality a religious rule? Again, no consensus exists on this point. It may be its presumed source: a command of a deity; its presence in an authorized sacred text; its conformity to sayings and actions of a paradigmatic religious person; its source in a larger theological framework from which it is a necessary, or at least reasonable, inference with reference to the activity of those who accept the framework. The same rule might well be adhered to by nonreligious persons; what makes it religious is the particularity of its authorization or backing. It may be shared but have a particular obligatory force because it is part of a particular religious way of life. Or, it may be a rule that is uniquely bound to its religious context, and adherence to it is seen as a matter of faithfulness to beliefs in that context. Thus it might not be justifiable on any other grounds than its theological or religious ones.

To offer a second illustration: human activity is goal oriented; this is a descriptive premise, like the assertion that human activity is rule governed. For example, negotiations between nation states to reduce chlorofluorocarbon emissions in the atmosphere has various proximate goals directed toward the reduction, if not elimination, of that pollutant. Health care plans are goal oriented; for example, they aspire to establish access to health care for all Americans. My conduct of a faculty seminar is goal oriented; it seeks to develop understanding and intelligibility across academic disciplines. Morality is continuous with these other forms of activity and experience. It is oriented toward the actualization of certain ideals or ends. This view certainly has historic, as well as philosophical backing.

Religious morality, according to some views, is also a morality of ends. Historical evidence supports this. Many religious communities aspire toward the realization or approximation of ideal ends. One hopes for the day when the lion and the lamb shall lie down together; another is oriented by the symbol of the realm of God, which might be specified in terms of the realization of peace, justice, and the integrity of creation, to cite World Council of Churches language. Another is oriented toward some end of human wholeness, of which physical and mental health are ingredients. Thus religious morality or ethics are continuous with ethics interpreted as a vision or system of ends.

What makes an end in religious morality a religious end? Again, there is no consensus on this point. For some, the end of being human, individually and communally, is the vision of God; the realization of moral ends and values is an ingredient of the process that leads to that end. For some, since God is the creator of the order of life, there is a coincidence between realizing a moral determination of our natural ends and the fulfillment of human good physically and socially. For some the end is the lure and authority of a figure in sacred history; conformity of life to the significance of that figure is the end.

The ends, like rules, might be widely shared, even though the reasons given by religious persons for their authority might be particular and distinctive. Or again, an end, such as holiness in classic Judaism, might have a very particular religious authorization and might require particular forms of action to fulfill it. Religious morality of ends is made intelligible by its continuities with other ethics of ends and with other human activities. The intelligibility makes religious ethics at least understandable, and maybe persuasive both within and outside the religious community.

The description, explanation, and interpretation of the nature of the human and of human activities offers a third illustration in anthropology. I mean *anthropology* in the classic sense: the morphology of humanity not only as distinct individual members but also as communities and a species. A decisive ingredient or dimension of every interpretation of economic, political, social, interpersonal experience, and of every commended or prescribed form of activity in these and other areas, is a descriptive anthropology. The description of the human in rational choice economics differs in some ways (though it may have similar outcomes) from that of sociobiology or psychoanalysis. In extrapolations from each of these descriptions to what is valued about life, there is coherence with the description of the human.

Morality is continuous with these endeavors and shares some of their features. Thus we have different moral anthropologies; Aristotle's is different from Kant's; Hobbes's is different from Rousseau's; that of some feminist ethics is different from that of some male-dominated ethics; that of enlightenment individualism in the West is different from that of Eastern traditions that stress the interdependence of humans with all things and thus a priority of a common good. The moral anthropology is intrinsic to the determination within various perspectives of what range of considerations is morally relevant, what evils are to be avoided and what goods sought, what restraints are necessary on human activity, and what aims are worthy of commendation or approval. Ethics, like economics and other forms of activity and intellectual endeavor, are based on one or another descriptive and explanatory account of the human—individuals, societies, and even species. This helps to make ethics intelligible.

What makes a moral anthropology a religious moral anthropology? Again, no consensus on this point exists. One answer would be that its source of knowledge is the revelation in sacred texts and in traditions that are particular to a religious community. Thus, one can appeal to the Genesis statement that humans are made in the image of God or to a Pauline text that stresses the universality of human sin. (I note that some economists have discovered "opportunism" and "the limits of rationality" to be sources of disturbance in economic activity and institutions. This sounds like a rediscovery of sin and finitude.) Or one can appeal to a biblical text that makes claims for the restorative and redeeming power of the Spirit.

The choice of a religious or theological backing for moral anthropology will affect how the moral life is interpreted: what is needed to restrain immorality or to sustain and enhance morality; what the ends of human life are within which the moral is an ingredient or dimension. If Christianity, for example, is finally about redemption or salvation, how morality and ethics are authorized and delineated has to be correlated or be coherent with their relations to faith and theology.

Different religious traditions have different moral anthropologies, and these can deeply affect the interpretation of the human and its relation to nature, to society, and to the future. One recalls, for example, Arthur Danto's *Mysticism and Morality*, which seems to argue that within Eastern religions, and particularly Hinduism, the view of the human does not make ethics possible in a Western sense. Or, among many statements of a commonly made generalization, Joseph Kitagawa argues that, "Eastern people have always accepted the humble role of being a part of the world of nature." He writes, "Gods proliferated, but they, like human beings and other beings, were subservient to the regulative order and inner balance of the cosmos, variously known as *Rta, Dharma,* and *Tao.*"[2] A larger and distinctive cosmological vision is the context for an anthropology; the moral anthropology is, at least in an ideal sense, saturated by this religious interpretation. The ethics that follow are framed and directed by the view of the human in the cosmos.

Moral or ethical visions or doctrines of the human are continuous with views of the human articulated for other purposes; religious moral visions of the human are made intelligible by showing their continuities with the concerns of any anthropology and by showing how the religion qualifies and adds distinctive dimensions to moral anthropology.

Again, application to religious medical ethics is not specified in this chapter; medicine has only been in the background. My general point is simple. Some literature in religious ethics makes such approaches intelligible both to members of religious communities and others by explaining or interpreting religious morality and ethics in continuity with other ethics. This might make religious ethics persuasive, particularly if they have the power to disclose dimensions and features of medical care and morality that are opaque from other perspectives. The intersection with medicine or other areas is crossed, like my first point, in application, in one direction: from the side of religious ethics.

Interaction

Interaction or dialectic between the proponents of autonomy and of intelligibility is taken up by Midgley in paragraphs that follow my quotation cited in note 1 of this chapter. This type is developed in other chapters of this book, as well as here. Some people within religious communities think that the explanation and interpretation of morals and the justification of ethics are interactive in a dialectical way. This might revise religious and theological affirmations that are made, as well as the ethics and their applications. The authorization is not the autonomy of religious ethics, nor is the effort confined to make religious ethics intelligible. The dialectical interaction attempts to move from intelligibility to some kind of justification. The recourse to religious language and symbols, and to theological language, it is hoped, broadens and deepens the interpretation of moral circumstances in medicine and elsewhere, and has some desirable outcome for the practices of morality in a human community more inclusive than those persons who can be socially identified as traditionally religious.

The interactional, dialectical process takes different forms and has different outcomes depending upon the content of the materials related to each other. From the standpoint of the autonomy type, for example, a religious view might shed distinctive light on human life, in medical and other circumstances, that is persuasive because of its disclosive power, or because its symbol forcefully defines a critical conviction that is deemed necessary on other than religious grounds. An example of this would be the symbol of humans being in the image of God. As a symbol of the intrinsic value of human beings and the respect due them regardless of particular conditions, the symbol is intelligible. Its authorization is particularistic but its significance is universal. And in turn, the moral appeal for intrinsic value of persons gives some authority to the symbol. The symbol's rhetorical power is not just its source in sacred text, but its wider moral meaning. What is authorized by the autonomy of religious ethics is made intelligible; it is explained both as to its source and its implications. But it is also justifiable on other grounds, and lends a kind of authority to its usage in a wider community of discourse.

In the case of the idea of the image of God, the dialectical interaction does not necessitate any revision of the religious principle. But whether the image of God is reducible to the moral principle of respect for persons is questionable, depending on what other features of the human theologians want to include in the image. And respect for persons can obviously be backed from Kantian or other views. In some circumstances, the religious symbol and the philosophical doctrine do not clash. In some other cases, they do, as in abortion debates and debates over death-delaying (usually called life-prolonging) therapies, where the judgments about qualities of personal or human existence differ.

A dialectic becomes critical for particular religious communities in a culture where there is no consensus about the theological or religious basis for respect for persons. In an essay, "The Sanctity of Life," Edward Shils states the continuing issues. The decline of Christian belief, he argues, is one of the major circumstances to be addressed in medical ethics: "The cognitive context of Christian doctrine, and above all the grandiose Christian symbolization of man's origin and destiny, have now lost much of their appeal." Shils proposes a replacement:

> The chief feature of the protoreligious, "natural metaphysic" is the affirmation that life *is* sacred. It is believed to be sacred not because it is a manifestation of a transcendent creator from whom life comes: it is believed to be sacred because it is life. The idea of sacredness is generated by the primordial experience of being alive, of experiencing the elemental sensation of vitality and the elemental fear of its extinction.

Thus Shils claims that life is sacred, "self-evidently." The practical task "is not so much the re-establishment of Christianity . . . but rather the rediscovery of what it was that for so long gave such persuasive power to Christianity."[3]

During the dominance of Christianity, the sanctity of life in our culture was explained by life's coming from God. It is really grounded, Shils argues, in a universal and primordial experience of being alive. This "self-evidence" needs further justification, so he proposes a "natural metaphysic" which he does not develop. For Shils this is not merely an interesting intellectual and historical matter; it is critical to sustaining the value of the human in a secular culture that tends to erode it. The traditional ethic is explained historically in terms of religion and also experientially; however, what he calls a natural metaphysic, or what might be called a naturalistic theology of nature, is also needed. The traditional religious backing has to be revised; the dialectic calls for changing the historic religious justification in order to be credible to many persons in our culture.

In the dialectical interaction between a religious explanation *and* justification of morality and ethics, and here particularly medical ethics, some religious writers can and do justify ethics by enlarging the scope of the "religious" so that persons no longer identified with historic religious communities can appreciate their own sense of the divine or sacred, and articulate it in nontraditional religious language, like Shils. The dialectic calls for a revision of the religious traditions and a broader interpretation of aspects of their significance.

Some persons, such as Mary Midgley, express this in a nonreductionist humanism. She writes,

> Humanism exists to celebrate and increase the glory of human life, undistracted for any entities outside it. But as soon as we begin to cut away those entities, valuable elements in human life itself start to go, too. The center begins to bleed. The patterns essential to human life turn out to be ones that cannot be altogether contained within it. They must, if given their full scope, lead far beyond it. To be fully human seems to involve being interested in other things as well as human ones, and sometimes more than human ones.[4]

This begins a section of her work titled "The Chimera of Self-Sufficiency." Beginning with the human, and moving toward all the conditions necessary for its well-being, one makes a powerful case against human self-sufficiency. It does not, for Midgley, lead to theology or traditional religion, but it extends the boundaries to territory also interpretable by theologies of creation or nature. The limits of self-sufficiency—surely a point of theological orthodoxy— justifies the expansion of the horizon to be accounted for.

It is in that common territory that interaction calls for, to some religious thinkers, an articulation of bases for common morality.

The effect of such an interactional-dialectical interpretation of a basis for ethics clearly does not resolve moral quandaries in their specificity. But it does provide a backing—both in terms of a moral stance or attitude and in terms of some general principles—from which persons strongly identified with a religious tradition and others can converse about medical morality. It can resonate with the *sensus divinitatis* that many persons have who are not identified with the practices of particular religious communities.

Each of these three typical ways of thinking has palpable limitations; something is gained and something is given up in each. While serious intellectual issues remain in arguing for the preference of one type over the other, in practice each is used, or all three may be used, depending upon the occasions in which religious ethicists are engaged with others about what is right and good in various medical practices and policies.

4 *Genetic Therapy: An Intersection of Science, Ethics, and Theology*

This chapter focuses on the ethical writings of Dr. W. French Anderson,[1] a very distinguished genetic therapist who clearly has religious sensibilities as well. This examination will reveal more clearly how scientific and clinical judgments intersect with ethical judgments and larger background beliefs about the human.

Literature on ethics and on developments in human genetics has a long and changing history, going back to proposals for eugenics that would presumably benefit the common good both by eliminating persons judged to be defective and by enhancing certain qualities in individuals judged to be of superior value. Since the rapid developments of bioethics in the past few decades, this literature has vastly expanded and continues to do so under the aegis of the Human Genome Initiative, which funded competitive grants dealing with legal, ethical, and social issues. The first prospect of cloning humans evoked a spate of literature to which philosophers and theologians contributed; recombinant DNA research brought more immediate possibilities under scrutiny; advancing development of genetic screening of parents and of newborn children raised fundamental issues about what is and ought to be valued about human life and thus what sorts of infants ought not to be born, as well as what therapies could be morally licit for children born with genetic defects.[2]

With the Human Genome Initiative new knowledge about human genetics expands at a dizzying rate. As a result of this very specific as well as more general knowledge, new opportunities for therapeutic interventions develop, such as Anderson's work with ADA, an immune-deficiency disease that affects children.

A new moral and public consciousness about therapeutic research in its experimental phases is evident, along with a notable sensitivity and sophistication about ethical issues on the part of many investigators. Some investigators might think that ethical regulations are a restraining externality, but for many, ethical sensitivity and sophistication are clearly matters of internal conviction and importance. Institutional frameworks both within the government and in the private sector now bring research and clinical experimentation into steady interaction with legal, ethical, and public concerns. Lawyers, theologians, and philosophers have learned enough science to grasp the specific quandaries faced by researchers and clinicians, and some of the latter have learned to use the vocabulary of ethics.

Anderson's publications are clear evidence of participation in this wider context of deliberation. An examination of his writings reveals how one genetic therapist thinks ethically. From this focus other considerations come to the fore; an expansion of the context makes this possible.

How Ethical Issues Are Formulated

What follows is my account of how I believe Anderson and other genetic therapists come to and formulate the ethical dimensions of their work. First, however, I would like to comment on how they do not.

Genetic therapists are not natural law theorists who draw inferences about the moral or religious legitimacy of certain interventions from a moral order of creation. Though they have background beliefs about the human as part of the evolutionary process, these do not dictate or determine their particular choices, although they may provide an aspect of them. The genetic therapists do not ordinarily come armed with a single-minded ethical theory that they have adopted as a result of their studies of moral philosophy—a theory that can rather deductively be applied to the case at hand. They have clearly been exposed to such theories, and are informed by them in stating the dimensions they perceive to be ethical, but normally do not adhere rigorously to one ethical theory. They know that they are dealing with the large and historically debated issue of what constitutes the distinctiveness and good, or goods, of the human. They are somewhat perplexed, as are most of us, about how health as a human good is related to other human goods, that is, in what ways it is a condition for other aspects of flourishing, or whether it comes near to being an end in itself. But, as Anderson's questions in his articles indicate, he and other genetic therapists do not have a simple coherent vision of the human good.

The process in which they engage is something like this. New knowledge coming from basic research gives insight into the causal factors involved in a genetically based human diseases. Thus, the possibility of new therapeutic interventions emerge. For both scientific and moral reasons, as Anderson and colleagues make clear, a sequence of laboratory research must precede the first use of a procedure on humans. With the best evidence in hand, they recognize the risk factors to human patients, and every bit of knowledge and care is used to minimize this risk and to maximize the desired healthy outcome. They adhere to the voluntary principle, requiring the properly informed consent of the patient or a proper surrogate. They distinguish between the purposes and biological conditions of genetic therapy; radical eugenics is ruled out for reasons given; enhancement therapy is at least questionable for given reasons; germ-line intervention, that is, interventions that would be transmitted to subsequent generations, might be justifiable in the future, but caution about this is strong; somatic cell therapy is licit given the accuracy of specific knowledge conditions for a particular disease.

Geneticists proceed with very cautious confidence to prepare a protocol that is justified by the scientific knowledge, the severity of the disease, the assessment of risks and other moral considerations, and the indication of the particular patient or patients for the experimental therapy. Follow-up procedures are clear and precise, and monitoring practices insure against both clinical and moral negligence on their part. They do not promise complete cures, but high probabilities of improved health. Thus medically and ethically they venture into a dimly lighted future; fallibility is recognized, but the evidence supports a clinical judgment that the intervention is worthy when a whole range of considerations are taken into account. They have decided that a particular intervention is good and right, medically and morally.

Because of the nature of their vocation, the focus of medical and ethical attention is on a particular act or a class of acts. The normal conditions of moral responsibility have been met, given certain background beliefs and assumptions of our culture and institutions. What can be done, in the case at hand, ought to be done. As I read Anderson, somatic cell genetic therapy, given proper knowledge conditions, ought to be done. But there are some interventions that, at least for the present, ought not to be done.

Put more formally, the steps toward a decision to undertake a procedure seem to answer the following questions: (1) What can be done now, given current knowledge conditions? (2) What ought to be done now, given this knowledge, and what reasons justify that? (3) What, in various scenarios of the future, are genetic therapists likely to be able to do? (4) What, in the light of present factors, scientific, ethical, and public responses, should and should not be done in each of those scenarios? (5) What reasons are given both for authorizing and for limiting possible interventions?

Different types of evidence or reasons are invoked to answer these questions. First, scientific knowledge conditions—current ones, those on the immediate horizon, and those that are probable in a more distant future—provide justification. Second are ethical guidelines and review procedures. These include boards and committees that must review all research proposals, such as assuring informed consent by the patient or a suitable surrogate, and a risk-benefit analysis with a judgment in favor of the benefits. They also include considerations of fairness or justice in access to therapy, the value of liberty that rules out coercive use, and concerns for various human goods—those that warrant therapy, those that do not, and those that are now ambiguous. Third, there are appeals to what the public will approve. And finally, there are larger beliefs about the human, what ought to be valued about human life, appeals to dignity, and so on, that are belief conditions on which there is not complete agreement.

Analysis of Anderson's ethical articles continues by lifting out the judgments made, proposed, or left open in each of these types of evidence as they move toward intersection in particular choices.

First, regarding *scientific knowledge conditions*, the standard procedures for preclinical trials are clearly necessary. Determination of when to begin clinical trials involves judgments about probabilities of success, but in the case of a tragic and lethal disease, he writes, "it would be just as inappropriate to delay treatment of patients while we are awaiting long-term results in primates as it would be to rush into experimentation with patients before studies of small animals have been completed."[3] Since genetic science is developing rapidly, the choice about what therapies to use in humans and under what conditions is an open, developing issue.

When the discussion moves from somatic cell therapies to germ-line, the knowledge conditions have to be specified differently: "It would require that we learn how to insert a genome not only into the appropriate cell of the patient's body, but also how to introduce it into the germ line of the patient in such a way that it would be transmitted to offspring and would be functional in the correct way in the correct cells in the offspring."[4] As of 1985, at least, the necessary technique, microinjecting a fertilized human egg, was not acceptable for three reasons: the procedure had a high failure rate (implying that a low enough failure rate might make it appropriate); it could produce a deleterious result (implying that when such a result can be avoided it might be appropriate), and it would have limited "usefulness" (again implying that when it would have greater usefulness it might be appropriate;[5] I will cite his ethical question below.

The knowledge conditions for some enhancement therapies seem to be in place, and more possibilities of this use of therapy will increase as human genetics develops. (The ethical questions raised by Anderson about enhancement therapy are intertwined with the knowledge conditions, discussed below.) The principal question is what constitutes a disease, and what constitutes prevention rather than enhancement.

Second, what *ethical considerations* are brought to bear to support judgments? As I noted, Anderson affirms the standard conditions that review committees must evaluate, that is, a favorable risk-benefit ratio and consent by the patient or a proper surrogate. In cases of tragic and lethal diseases, when experimental therapy might be done without the scientific certainty normally required, the possible preservation of life overrides normal constraints. Here ethical thinking is somewhat similar to thinking in the just-war tradition; when all nonviolent means to settling a dispute have been attempted, given the conditions of a just cause, violence might be reasonable. The medical-ethical warrant implied by Anderson is not new; the crisis of impending, but possibly avoidable, death warrants extreme measure. Some critics view this warrant to be a justification for experiments that could be unethical on other principles. One is impressed, however, by the careful assessment of the risks, and the acknowledgment of the seriousness of the medical judgment that has to be made.

The ethical questions Anderson raises about germ-line therapy imply consideration of several values and concerns. One is irreversibility of outcomes; an inherited change could perpetuate any mistake. Another is unanticipated outcomes. At this point the Catholic moral theological procedures of the principle of double (or multiple) effect could be invoked. (Indeed, something like this procedure of reasoning seems implied in Anderson's other moral evaluations.) A stringent response can be inferred, or is at least suggested by Anderson. Any germ-line therapy ought to be restrained until there is a high probability that deleterious outcomes not now foreseeable will not occur. This, I take it, would apply even if the foreseeable outcomes also were beneficial to the patient and his or her progeny. One is not quite sure how Anderson would deal with this since it is raised as a critical ethical *question* and not precisely answered.[6]

The conditions that would warrant enhancement therapy are clear: they "could be justified on grounds of preventive medicine."[7] His well-chosen example relates to atherosclerosis, and the case is strong unless there was some alternative therapy that did not involve genetic enhancement of the conditions described. The line between enhancement and prevention, however, is not always drawn as easily. A somewhat analogous situation is purely cosmetic surgery. The argument that it can *enhance* self-esteem, enable better performance in the competitive marketplace, and so on, can be made in the following way. It *prevents* loss of self-esteem, which is a necessary condition for human flourishing, including flourishing in the marketplace. The difference between Anderson's example and this one is clear: his involves a physical disease for which the therapy would result in a more normal functioning of the body. Cosmetic surgery is justified by certain cultural values that are used to judge oneself or to judge other persons. Anderson does discuss growth hormones, which come closer to the example of cosmetic surgery. There he leaves us with a question of its appropriateness: "Should a pubescent adolescent whose parents are both five feet tall be provided with a growth hormone on request?"[8]

These examples point to the very large question of what are the proper ends of medicine, a question raised sharply by Leon Kass's much-cited article, "Regarding the End of Medicine and the Pursuit of Health."[9] The deep, perplexing questions are whether the purpose of medicine is only to remedy impediments to more "normal" bodily functions, or also to enhance some normal functions. What constitutes "normal"? Is the normal derived somehow from the "natural"? For example, if the use of the growth hormone in Anderson's example were withheld, would that be justified on the grounds that being relatively short is for that adolescent going to be natural, and therefore normal, and therefore it is wrong to use the hormone? I shall return to some of these larger issues of belief later. Anderson raises this issue when he asks what distinguishes a "serious disease" from a "minor disease from a cultural discomfort"[10]

Anderson also invokes the issue of fairness or justice in gaining access to genetic therapy, and particularly to enhancement therapy. His question is "How to determine who should receive a gene?"[11] The more specific questions are those that have been raised about access to scarce medical resources in the past. Should the persons be those who can most benefit society? Those most in need medically, to avoid significant suffering and premature death? Those who are able to pay? Or should the treatment be doled out by casting lots? It would be redundant to develop these questions more; there are much-cited studies of various answers to them.

Anderson also articulates the issue of avoiding discrimination. Again the specific issues are those that arise from any genetic screening. For example, will persons be deprived of health insurance if they are not treated? Will certain persons be coerced into forms of enhancement therapy in a time of national crisis presumably for the sake of the public good? The value of individual autonomy is invoked against any arguments that would justify coercion even for the sake of a public good.[12] It is clear that the larger vision of a good society that backs this is one based on individual liberties. Whether there would ever be "emergency" circumstances that would override individual autonomy seems to be ruled out.

Another kind of ethical argument that Anderson invokes is the "slippery slope." He writes, "It would be difficult, if not impossible, to determine where to draw a line once enhancement engineering had begun. Therefore, gene transfer should be used only for treatment of serious disease and not for putative improvements."[13] In a sense we are on a slippery slope already with the capacities to engage in genetic therapy. As on other such slopes a site is located beyond which we ought not to go. Some things ought not be done even though they can be done. Anderson's line between serious disease and "putative improvements" was commented on above; what is the basis for drawing the distinction he has made?

Third, Anderson suggests the *importance of public approval* of possible germ-line interventions.[14] He indicates that what the public approves changes over time. Thus part of the medical-ethical strategy is to educate the public to gain its approval for therapies that are possible, as well as medically and ethically legitimate. Presumably a corollary of this is to gain support for discussion of problematic possibilities and perhaps for drawing a firm line against some of them. There is a broadening context of discussion; experimental germ-line therapies are not matters to be agreed upon between only the physician and his or her patients or appropriate surrogates, as decisions about surrogate motherhood are.

Anderson does not consider the important practical question of how medically and ethically informed public discussion is to take place. Authors who have attracted wide public attention, such as Nicholas Wade and Jeremy Rifkin, are cited for their alarms about the potential abuse of power that might slide down the slope to eugenics. Anderson's rhetorical question—"But are they really that far off the mark?"[15]—sounds somewhat sympathetic toward them. I raise the practical question because it is easier for prophetic alarmists to gain public attention than for persons who are prudently complex about both the medical and moral dimensions. Genetic therapy is just one example of a larger issue in our society: how is an adequately informed public opinion to be developed on critical and controversial issues? Do we have institutions and processes in place for this to occur?

One of Anderson's discussions of germ-line therapy contains an intriguing claim. "The gene pool is a joint possession of all members of society," and it would be affected by outcomes of germ-line therapy.[16] This backs his concern for public discussion and approval. Anderson does not discuss the probabilities of long-range beneficial or deleterious outcomes in the gene pool in specific ways. *Possession* is a term that suggests a legal structure invoking laws of property, with implications of a location of authority, somewhere, to determine its lawful use. The ramifications of this are great socially, legally, and ethically. Who is the guardian of the gene pool? By what authority? What powers does the guardian have? How are they to be exercised?

Fourth, and finally as a point of reflection on Anderson's writings, there are appeals to *profound background conditions*, more belief conditions than scientific knowledge conditions. They are opened by some of Anderson's questions: What constitutes human dignity? What is significant suffering? What is normal? His 1989 article, particularly, cites a breadth of literature by ecclesial authors and groups, by moral theologians and ethicists, and others who do move the discussion to these perplexing questions. As I noted earlier, Anderson does not seek to resolve them, but is clearly conscious of them.

In this analytical description of French Anderson's ethical writings we see that scientific information is the necessary condition for clinical judgments, but that clinical judgments require consideration of other factors as well. Some of these considerations are quite precise: standards of informed consent that recognize the autonomy of the patient must be followed. The assessment of risks and benefits has to be as precise as possible, and in cases of significant doubt about future outcomes, restraint is required except in life-threatening circumstances. Under these circumstances the imperative to save life overrides uncertainty about scientific knowledge conditions.

Anderson uses rhetorical questions in many places to open both quite specific issues and more general ones. For example, the distinction between prevention and enhancement raises the question of whether diseases that threaten physical health are the only justification for intervention, or whether personal and cultural values can justify it. In effect, Anderson very understandably has not determined what sources of knowledge, what values and principles, what concepts override others when a clinical choice has to be made. He may be practicing a process of discernment, which is not reducible to moral geometry or syllogisms, and this might well be the wisest course.

Description and Evaluation: A Postscript

I have alluded to how Anderson's discussions of the ethics of genetic therapy move to margins of larger and more controverted issues about the nature of the human and human activity. Although he does not address connections in detail, issues of what are biologically natural, biologically normal, and ethically normative are somehow related in his work. These matters show particularly in his assessments of enhancement therapy.

Anderson's ethical writings are another locus of matters examined in the introduction and particularly in chapter 1 of this book. The latter showed how two authors, Edward O. Wilson and Melvin Konner, begin with what humans most share with other animals, and indeed with all living things. Two other authors, Abraham Heschel and Reinhold Niebuhr, begin with what they perceive to be the most radically distinctive, indeed unique, characteristic of the human. Chapter 5 frames in a somewhat different way the intersections of biology, theology, and ethics.

From novels and dramas to biology, biophysics, and chemistry, literature provides the analyst with answers to four questions, at least by implication, and with clues to the relations made or assumed between the answers. The questions are: How is the distinctively human described, explained, and interpreted? What is valued about the human? What ought to be valued about it? And how are descriptions, explanations, and interpretations on the one hand and valuations on the other hand, related to each other? The disciplinary or experiential contexts in which these questions are asked affect which information, concepts, and modes of argumentation are featured. Polarities abound; nature-nurture and others have been listed previously. Comparative analysis of even a small portion of relevant literature is beyond the scope of this book. We proceed within the bounds of theology, biology, and ethics.

5 *Theology, Biology, and Ethics: Further Explorations*

hapter 4 focused on an example of the intersection of genetics and ethics, and some of the implications of that intersection for wider theological and philosophical issues. This chapter continues that exploration, distinguishing between two intersections more clearly: what I call the moral intersection and the theological intersection. The writings of a few important authors are sufficient to raise more general matters that are worthy of attention.

The Moral-Scientific Intersection

The moral intersection received primary attention in chapter 4. The questions that Dr. W. French Anderson raised about genetic therapy are typical. Given present and future knowledge conditions, what procedures are morally defensible and which are morally questionable? Where there is moral ambiguity, how does a responsible investigator, physician, or community make a choice? What ends are worthy? What criteria are invoked to guide both restraints and interventions? At this intersection theologians, moral philosophers, genetic therapists and other physicians, playwrights, and a lot of the wider public function as practical moralists. A case, or a class of cases, focuses discussion, and procedures for making moral judgments are used to defend their choices or to highlight ambiguities often by asking rhetorical questions.

Clinicians and experimenters, like policymakers, tend to begin with these questions: What is going on? What possible courses of action do present knowledge and resource conditions make possible? These frame the discussions of ethics and even set parameters within which various insights or theories of ethics are used. The intersection between medicine and ethics is traversed in both directions, and the choice is often a combination that has to be justified by evidence and concepts from both the relevant science and ethics.

In contrast to this apparent procedure many moral philosophers and moral theologians start with an ethical theory, or with theological beliefs as relatively independent from the matters to which they will subsequently be addressed. The preference, which is intellectually justified, is for the autonomy of ethics, theological or philosophical, and thus the traffic at the intersection moves dominantly, if not exclusively, from the ethical and theological to the experimental and clinical.

In this chapter I explore the ways in which some beliefs, particularly theological ones, that are held independently of various specific moral contexts, predispose persons to adopt particular arguments and make particular judgments. While genetics is the source of most examples, by analogy the discussion would be applicable to other areas of experimentation and intervention, and to matters of judgment about social and economic policies as well.

One set of background beliefs pertains to how human nature is to be interpreted; different interpretations provide backing for quite specific moral judgments. Specifically, how do authors who rely on traditional Christian theology support approaches to the ethics of genetic research and therapy?[1]

I turn to Paul Ramsey's memorable aphorism: "[Human beings] ought not to play god before they learn to be [human beings], and after they have learned to be [human beings] they will not play God."[2] What seem to be the theological presuppositions of this aphorism? Why should human beings not "play god"? Because human beings are finite. Whatever their capacities for increasing both the knowledge of biological life and controlling its development, they will never have complete foreknowledge of the outcomes of their interventions in nature and never have complete control of their consequences. While Ramsey does not develop a doctrine of God in this context, he implies that in contrast to God, to be human is to be limited in knowledge and in power; to be God is to be omniscient and omnipotent.

Ramsey's aphorism is similar to Karl Barth's persistent warnings in his "Protection of Life." Barth asserts that humans ought never to "usurp the divine prerogatives" that ultimately determine the destiny of human lives.[3]

The following outlook contends that restraints in seeking to control human destiny, at least genetically, are prudent. This attitude of restraint, of course, can be backed by other observations and arguments. Theology has no monopoly on the wisdom that is counseled. Although knowledge increases and with it the capacities intentionally to direct the course of human life, humans still work within significant limitations of both knowledge and power. Boundaries exist to limit even the best-informed efforts to calculate the probabilities of outcomes of various proposals for intervention. Ramsey would not be caught giving "a priestly blessing over everything" that is scientifically and technologically possible. When human beings learn to be human they will not play God.

In addition to recognition of human finitude, the propensity to moral evil, which all humans are believed to share, is another facet of many theological interpretations of human nature. How theologians make judgments about particular genetic experiments and interventions is related, at least indirectly, to where they stand on a continuum of the effects of human sinfulness. A theologian who believes in the thoroughness of human corruption is likely to attribute to geneticists motives and perspectives that are the result of pride; that are self-serving (such as engaging in experiments and procedures because they are technically possible and might win acclaim); that are Promethean, such as Edward O. Wilson celebrates in the last paragraph of his *On Human Nature*;[4] or that are reductionistic in the sense that the human becomes simply a biological organism with no distinct inherent respect or mystery to be honored in it. Each of these might be forms of the "technological imperative," the drive to increase human control over life in general and over the destiny of particular persons. That imperative not only outruns the limits of finitude, but also represents an extraordinarily powerful form of human sinfulness: arrogance, pride, and the lust for power.

Ramsey's aphorism is followed by his attack on Karl Rahner's article, "The Experiment with Man," which Ramsey says "sounds remarkably like a priestly blessing over everything, doing duty for ethics." Rahner's argument in that article has to be set in the context of his more inclusive philosophy and theology to be properly interpreted, something Ramsey does not undertake. Rahner's next article, "The Problem of Genetic Manipulation," shows sharp limits to what he would condone, but does illustrate how different theological interpretations of the "essence" (nature, in one sense) of the human affect dispositions toward human intervention in genetics; its subtitle is "Theological Observations on Man's Self-Manipulation." Rahner is responding to what he calls Catholic "traditional text-book moral theology," that has "often used a concept of 'nature' ('natural,' 'according to nature') which ignores the fact that, although man has an essential nature which he must respect in all his dealings, man himself is a being who forms and molds his own nature through culture, i.e., in this case through self-manipulation, and he may not simply presuppose his nature as a categorical, fixed quantity."[5]

The essence of the human, for Rahner, is radical, "transcendental" freedom; by divine appointment humans have "the commission and the power" that enable them "to be free to determine" themselves—ultimately and most importantly, for Rahner, to determine their "final state" in relation to God. But this same freedom takes on a historical form in modern culture; as biological and historical beings, it provides the conditions for increased powers of human self-manipulation. What modern genetics enables is continuous with other forms of interventions: medicine, social planning, political organization, and so on. By accenting, in this essay, freedom as the essential nature of humans more than the conditions of human finitude and sin (though these are clearly present), Rahner suggests an outlook of openness to experimentation and intervention: "[M]an's active intramundane self-planning in self-manipulation has fundamentally a positive relationship to man's openness to the absolute future in faith and hope."[6]

Rahner is not without words of caution, even in this essay. He recognizes that the outcomes of self-manipulation can be both beneficial and bad for the human futures. The self-manipulation, normatively, ought never to run counter to human essence, that is, freedom. A wider theological perspective backs his ultimate confidence in the human future and warns against penultimate evils: "Jubilation or lamentation would both run counter to the Christian's cool-headedness." The Christian "has no reason to enter the future as a hell on Earth nor as an earthly Kingdom of God."[7] The wider theology has confidence that nature and human activity are finally under the direction of divine grace, and that harmful excesses in self-manipulation will be recognized and corrected in the course of human developments. Put theologically, Rahner's eschatology, his confidence in the power of divine grace and goodness to prevail and to sustain the realization of human life, supports his nonalarmist view of genetic and other experiments with humans.

These examples show how different theologies support attitudes toward genetic intervention; these attitudes, however, do not *determine* the precise moral judgments about particular procedures. Ramsey writes, "Thus a Christian, as such, intends the world as God intends the world," and God intends the world with love. Rahner probably would not disagree with that. Ramsey chooses to stress ethics of means based on the idea of covenant to apply to genetic interventions; Rahner's is more, but not exclusively, an ethic of ends. The dignity of the human for Ramsey "consists not only in thought" or in "freedom"; there are other "elements in the nature of man which are deserving of respect and should be withheld from human handling or trespass."[8] While he recognizes that errors will be made in inculpable ignorance, he adopts the Pauline injunction that humans ought to avoid doing evil for the sake of good ends.

The classic idea of humans being made in the image of God is relevant. J. Robert Nelson, for example, in his *biblically* theological treatise on bioethics, writes that, "Humanness is the distinctive quality implied by the symbol of 'the image of God,' the image in which everyone is created and which is the presupposition of life's meaning; everyone's unique identity is the creation and endowment of God."[9] For him, and for most authors who invoke that biblical symbol, it functions to posit a reality in all humans that gives them intrinsic value, making them worthy of ultimate and inviolable respect. Generally, the symbol is invoked as a limit to human intervention, supporting an ethics of restraint.

What the image is asserted to be, however, makes a difference in its possible backing for or against particular interventions. If the image is the soul, and if the soul is conceived to have independence from the body, then no genetic interventions can affect it, though it would not follow from this that geneticists would have license to do what they please with the body. If the image is destroyed, or defaced by human sin, that could affect the extent to which geneticists are trustworthy stewards of anything that affects the human. Since the image is of God, what is permitted or prohibited will be affected by what conception of God is operative.

For example, if God is the absolutely free creative agent who has power to do what God wills, and creativity is God's image in humans, "playing god" might be converted into imitating God. The human capacities to be creative, to act, to exercise dominion over nature, could be blessed, and the expansion of genetic control supported. If God is spoken of in terms of gracious goodness for humanity, in a Barthian sense, the parameters within which intervention is permitted will depend on inferences drawn from what is the divine good for the human. In many instances, I believe the use of the idea of the image of God as a basis for ethics becomes circular; what God is imaged to be is what is distinct about the human, or what is claimed to be distinct about the human is projected onto God. To invoke the symbol to support specific moral judgments requires a series of intervening steps that are not strictly theological.

In these examples the intersection is basically between genetics, theology, and theological ethics; these draw upon traditional Christian theological beliefs, some quite confessional in a biblical sense, and others interpreted more philosophically. Except possibly in the case of Karl Rahner, knowledge of genetics is not important theologically, that is, it is not decisive in the interpretation of the human, or of the Divine. Rahner does seem to open the possibility of further exploration of how genetic knowledge would affect the category within which the transcendental freedom is imbedded, and his confidence in the ultimate power of di-

vine grace provides a tentatively stated assurance that deleterious interventions would be corrected in the processes of
cultural development. Basically, for Ramsey and other authors, biological, and particularly genetic, information describes and interprets sets of circumstances within which
human choices are made. It is morally relevant in the sense
that a responsible moral choice has to take account of the
courses of action this information makes possible, and the
likely alternative outcomes. However, Ramsey offers an
inkling of one qualification in this regard when he writes
that the dignity of the human involves not only thought and
freedom but other elements in the nature of the human.

I make the point, perhaps too strongly, by saying that the
traffic across the intersection from theology and theological
ethics is one way, from what theology affirms to the experimental or clinical biological and genetic circumstances to
which its insights are ethically applied. There is little or no
traffic from the scientific to the theological; the theological
is not reinterpreted in any significant way as a result of the
scientific knowledge. Plainly, however, it is not necessary,
for example, to invoke a contrast between God and the
human to make the point that humans are not omniscient
or omnipotent. We have seen that, without invoking theology, Dr. W. French Anderson (and many others) acknowledge constraints on their activity because of limits of
knowledge, foreknowledge, and the power to fully control
outcomes, both immediate and long range. Science provides
probabilities and not certitudes of outcomes. Scientists do
not need to contrast the human with God to make this point;
observations of the limits of the human are sufficient.

Geneticists are not armed, or burdened, with a tradition
that disposes them to worry about usurping the divine prerogatives, or about how deep the effect of the human fault
is, or about what the image of God in humans is. Theology
is not a source for the symbols they use to interpret nature,
including human nature. But the range of concerns about

the ethics of genetic intervention is as broad as that of theologians. Some events can be recalled to make the point: the famous Asilomar conference on recombinant DNA research; the development of federal regulations governing that activity and their subsequent revision; the establishment of an ethics committee to review research proposals in this area, etc.

Outlooks of scientists, like those of theologians and others, have differed as a result of different background beliefs about the human. These beliefs can be inferred, if they are not explicitly stated. Some scientists, like many who now strongly support the Human Genome Initiative, foresaw enormous beneficial outcomes for humanity—not only the relief of human suffering in individuals, but collective benefits for society and even the gene pool. Others, like some theologians, expressed apocalyptic anxieties about possible misuses of genetic knowledge. While differences abound in scientific judgments about what is worth knowing, how fast knowledge will accrue, and what interventions will be possible and when, differences can also be attributed to various moral and even (in a generic sense) religious or background beliefs.

The question, In whom or what can human beings trust? has different implied, if not articulated, answers. Ought we to have confidence in the moral and social intentions of those who have access to this knowledge, and those who will make choices about how it will be used? Or ought we to be wary, to say the least, and take into account possible corruptions of the use of knowledge, and possible long-range deleterious effects on the species and on societies?

The question, For what can human beings hope? has different answers. If not outright utopian, nearly utopian aspirations have been expressed. Knowledge will enable the avoidance of some pain and suffering, and make possible, for example, the prolongation of life when the genetics of aging can be explained. Some scientists have claimed benefits for society, even through projections of economic factors. Others emphasize what we should fear about the possible future. Implicitly, and sometimes explicitly, the question is, What is to be valued about human life? Underlying that is the deeper question, How is what we value related to some notion of the nature of human life? Is longevity to be valued in itself, or even as a condition for other valued aspects of human life? What are those? Is aging "natural" and thus to be accepted like death must be? Or is aging a disease that warrants intervention, and thus abnormal with reference to some inchoate reference of the natural?

I cannot resist quoting again the peroration of Edward O. Wilson's *On Human Nature*:

> The human species can change its own nature. What will it choose? Will it remain the same, teetering on a jerrybuilt foundation of partly obsolete Ice-Age adaptations? Or will it press on toward still higher intelligence and creativity, accompanied by a greater—or lesser— capacity for emotional response? . . . It might be possible to imitate genetically the more nearly perfect nuclear family of the white-handed gibbon or the harmonious sisterhood of the honeybees. But we are talking here about the very essence of humanity.[10]

My point is that what a biologist believes about the very nature or essence of humanity, and what he or she posits as the distinctive values of that essence, will affect what experimentation and therapy he or she would support. The regulative idea of the nature of the human, a background belief not derived from science alone, is a critical factor not only for theologians, but also for geneticists, as it affects their moral outlooks and judgments.

I can again note two areas of possible genetic interventions where some ambiguous appeals to the naturally normal as a ground for the morally normative seem to function in discussions. The first is aging, already mentioned. In arguments against intervening, once the genetics of aging is known more precisely, appeals are made to outcomes for social policies due to the changing age distribution of the population, as well as to the fact that aging is a part of biological nature, just as death is. "Nature"—aging, in this case—is in some sense "normal" in the latter argument, and thus a source of norms, so intervention into the aging process ought to be prohibited.

The second area involves the discussion of genetic enhancement therapy. Therapy that is intended to relieve impairments of various human functions—that is, if "enhancement" is a preventive procedure—assumes something abnormal (unnatural?) about the condition, making therapy morally licit. However, resistance to the "improvement" of memory, intelligence, height, and other human features leads to ambiguous appeals to the natural being normal and thus a basis for different ethical judgments.

Why do scientists draw from sources other than science when they consider what ought to be done? One answer is that they value many aspects of human life and other parts of nature. They have aesthetic appreciations and moral beliefs or aspirations—grounded only in part in their scientific work—which, to a scholar of religion, function much like myths, doctrines, and practices of religion in various human cultures. These beliefs cross the intersection of work done by theologians and other humanists. At the intersections, with prognoses of hope or fear even when confined to particular genetic interventions, both geneticists and religious thinkers are providing answers to the questions of what is valued about human life, and about particular human lives, and thus what ought and ought not to be done. The recurring systematic question is the relation of what is valued to the biologically natural or normal. This is a question for both theologians and geneticists.

The Theological-Scientific Intersection

The second intersection I call theological-scientific. The questions are these: What do theologians make of genetic and other scientific knowledge in their interpretations of how God created and is ordering life in the world, including human life? Does "nature," as created by God and informed by genetics, enter into the theologian's ethical judgments? Further, how do geneticists and other biologists, who move beyond the strict entailments of their sciences to explore the meaning and purpose of human life, support those moves to what are religious affirmations, or at least the functional equivalents of them? What sources and premises do they use and elide in this process of becoming, in some sense, natural theologians, or theologians of nature?

To the first of these two sets of questions, theologians answer on a spectrum of possibilities from bracketing genetic knowledge out of serious theological consideration to building their theologies by presumably rational inferences from it. Between the extremes are various ways of incorporating genetic knowledge, some of which will be noted, as an explication of the divine ordering of nature and as providing both enabling and limiting conditions for human life that are morally and theologically important.

The work of some Protestant theologians can illustrate the bracketing out of genetic knowledge at the scientific-theological intersection. First, Paul Ramsey, whose contributions to the ethical intersection are very important, nowhere to my knowledge undertakes to show the importance of genetics for understanding nature, or "creation" as theologians prefer to call it, and for a theological interpretation of nature. Ramsey certainly knew enough genetics to analyze intelligibly the cases that had to be addressed by his theological ethics. But his theological ethics are based on the idea of covenant and Christian love, and he developed procedures of casuistry grounded in them to make choices about particular interventions. Because, in my judgment, Ramsey's theology did not expound "nature" in a serious way (did not refer seriously to the first article of the Apostle's Creed, for the theologically initiated), he does not really cross the intersection between genetic science and theology. Nor does he address what genetics informs us about nature, and its significance for a theological and ethical interpretation of human nature. Covenant and love, rather than creation and nature, are the theological bases of his ethics. Nature and genetics are things to which theological ethics are applied, not sources of theological and ethical knowledge.

My second example illustrates how a theologian can first bracket out what genetics can inform about the human, and then permit it to come back in when it is interpreted in the light of biblical theological claims. I have in mind Karl Barth's discussion of the "real" and "phenomenal" humans. "Real" man, to use Barth's word, is the person in relation to God. The phenomenal human is informed by various naturalistic explanatory accounts of life. Knowledge of the real man comes from the revelation of the divine goodness toward the human in Jesus Christ, and from the human capacities to be responsive and responsible in relation to God. Genetics, like the matters of biology, psychology, and other disciplines Barth discusses, never tells us anything about the *real* nature of the human, about our freedom to be for God. In this respect one is reminded of Rabbi Heschel's sentence, "We can attain adequate understanding of man only if we think of man in human terms, *more humano*, and abstain from employing categories developed in the investigation of lower forms of life."[11]

However, once we know what Barth intends as the true nature of the human, the "real man," the sciences give us "real indications of the human. We can now affirm that all scientific knowledge of man is not objectively empty, but that it has a real object." He writes, "What natural science sees and tries to understand and present as man may certainly be a symptom of his true nature." The symptom can be interpreted in the light of the revelation of God, but cannot be a source of the knowledge of God.[12] This is somewhat similar to how J. Robert Nelson (see above) applies the independent authority of a biblical theology to the independent authority of biology in order to interpret the meaning of the latter and to draw ethical conclusions from that interpretation.

In contrast with the above examples, are there theologians for whom genetic and other scientific knowledge is, if not a source for knowledge of God, at least one body of information that has to be taken into account in interpreting God? Of course there are, and throughout Western theology they have appealed to understandings of nature in order to understand how God orders, sustains, and directs natural events and humans as natural beings. Whether the "Book of Nature" is a sufficient source for knowledge of God, or if it is not a sufficient source, how current scientific knowledge contributes to a construal of God, have been debated questions for centuries.

Two shapers of modern theology can be cited to show the importance of taking the sciences into consideration. First, Ernst Troeltsch writes:

> The idea of God is admittedly not directly accessible in any other way than by religious belief. Yet it asserts a substantial content which must stand in harmony with the other forms of scientific knowledge and also be in some way indicated by these.

Second, Paul Tillich writes:

> Of course, theology cannot rest on scientific theory. But it must relate its understanding of man to an understanding of universal nature for man is part of nature and statements about nature underlie every statement

about [man]. . . . Even if the questions about the relation
of man to nature and to the universe could be avoided by
theologians, they would still be asked by people of every
place and time—often with existential urgency and out
of cognitive honesty. And the lack of answer can become
a stumbling block for man's whole religious life.[13]

Note the different terms used in these quotations, which
would warrant different authority to genetics and other sciences for constructions or interpretations of the relations
of the Divine to the human and to nature at large: "Cannot
rest upon . . . , but must relate its understanding to . . . universal nature"; "must stand in harmony with and also
be . . . indicated by" forms of scientific knowledge. Neither
of these quotations authorizes a deductive process from scientific information and theories to a doctrine of God. Neither of them assumes that evidence from the sciences is sufficient to sustain belief in God. Both are somewhere
between the extremes of a continuum. I have suggested
one end of that continuum above, namely that belief in and
knowledge of God must be biblically based. The other end is
that, for example, God is natural selection, a position stated
by Ralph Wendell Burhoe.[14] Troeltsch's "must stand in
harmony with . . ." is clearly a stronger claim than Tillich's
"must relate its understanding to . . ."

Different scientific sources will have particular reference to different aspects of any theology of nature or creation. One focus of attention is on the human, per se; how
do various sciences of the human, those that explain us biologically as well as those that interpret us psychologically
and socially, affect the development of a theological anthropology? Another is how do explanations and interpretations of more universal aspects of nature affect our theological understandings of the place of the human in the
much larger scheme of things? Answers to these questions
are proposed not only by theologians but also by scientists

who begin to speculate beyond the immediate and verifiable conclusions of their professional efforts. I first turn to some very recent writings by American theologians that specifically and explicitly seek to inform theology by biology, each of which is somewhere in the middle between the poles stated above. Each of the authors is concerned to overcome faults they perceive in the work of others; all that I use focus on the human, but are concerned with the relation of the human to wider natural processes.

The first is the work of Stephen J. Pope, a Roman Catholic moral theologian, which I believe can be summarized as follows. Given the theological conviction that God is the creator, and that there is a divine ordering in and through nature that directs it toward good ends, or at least that cannot be grossly violated without peril to humans and the rest of nature, genetics and other aspects of biology provide a modern description, explanation, or interpretation of that divine ordering. Put more generally, if one accepts fundamental assumptions of theological natural law, and if one judges that in Thomas Aquinas and the classic Catholic tradition that law was explicated in terms of Aristotelian science, including biology, it should be possible to introduce modern biology and genetics to replace the Aristotelian sciences used in the past to interpret, ultimately, the divine ordering of nature.

Pope's work is motivated by perceived insufficiencies in recent Roman Catholic interpretations of life that stress excessively the personalism characteristics of loving relations. These efforts themselves were in part reactions against the "biologism" or "physicalism" that militated against understanding of persons in terms formulated by phenomenological and existentialist views, and have their own coherence with Christian themes. The central issue is one we have met before in this book. When we talk about the "nature" of persons do we refer to distinctive capacities for, for example, responsiveness and freedom, or do we refer to that other part of human nature which Aquinas described as what we share with all other living things?

Pope focuses on the ordering of love as developed by Aquinas, which permitted graded obligations to others and made possible quite precise moral distinctions and evaluations. Pope's central hypothesis is that this ordering of loves can be fruitfully reinterpreted by using knowledge and hypotheses from sociobiology and other aspects of biology. After careful discussion of sociobiology, attending to its complexities and ambiguities in the claims of various contributors to it, he uses kin-selection theory as an example.

> If we can grant with Thomas that moral values are based on natural inclinations, we can draw on sociobiological information and insights into our natural preferences for kin to illumine one important arena of moral value. Kin selection can play an important role not only in understanding natural preferences, but also in morally authorizing the giving of moral priorities to care of close family members. Restating Thomas' naturally based order of charity in an evolutionary context, we can argue that kin altruism, like other natural inclinations, reflects the divine ordering.[15]

Pope is more nuanced than this quotation and summary indicate. What is significant for this chapter is that from his use of some contemporary sciences he crosses the intersection to theology; the sciences of the human reflect the divine ordering. Both the divine ordering and the human are reinterpreted in the light of scientific material. Thus a kind of theological naturalism, a theological interpretation of nature, becomes the naturalistic basis for some aspects of ethics, the ordering of human inclinations. We reason from and about these inclinations, seeking to give them a morally proper ordering.

Philip Hefner has recently published a much more inclusive and synthetic account of *The Human Factor*. Again I cite only portions of it that pertain to the theme under discussion here.

> Inasmuch as the information necessary to construct the human being, as well as the actual processes of development and the environment in which humans have arisen, are what we call the realm of nature, whatever humans do in their culture-creating and culture-enacting must be referred to the natural order that is their source and ambience. . . . God's will for us humans transpires within the larger realm of the divine will for the entire natural order, as creation. . . . I argue that whatever it means for humans to find fulfillment, which certainly includes love, justice, peace, and the like, that fulfillment must be defined within the larger framework of the natural order.

Nature is the matrix of being human, and nature is "God's great project." Hefner writes, "For theology, this entails the conclusion that theology is not on track unless it can interpret the traditions of the religious communities as revelation about the natural order." Perhaps something like Tillich's statement, quoted above, Hefner's does not propose that theology "rests" on scientific theory, but that it must "relate" to it. He does not propose that science gives knowledge of God, per se, but affirms that "God-talk should be viewed as expressing something about our experience of a world that is scientifically understood."[16] Theology has an interpretive task, more than an explanatory one; it expresses the meaning of our experience in the world. Hefner adduces sayings of Jesus as a basis for "contextualizing" the scientific interpretations in a God-centered way of living in the world.

Again, in Hefner's work the crossing is not from dogmatic theology to the sciences; rather the sciences provide contemporary and reliable understandings of the natural order of which we are a part. More generally than Stephen

Pope, in my judgment, he implies that we learn about the divine ordering of the human and its context in the wider order of nature from the sciences. There is a crossing from sciences to theology, but the task of theology is a larger interpretive one of providing a coherent interpretation of a God-centered universe within which we find appropriate forms of life. The natural ordering is the context and basis for determining appropriate forms of life and some specific activities. Ethics will be based, at least in part, on a scientific understanding of nature.

My third example is from Edward Farley's *Good and Evil: Interpreting the Human Condition*. One of his basic queries is how to bring together the biological and personal aspects of being human into a more coherent and unified framework. The options he develops are similar to those used in this chapter: "the human being described by the sciences is the real human being"; "theology describes the real human condition and what the sciences are studying and discovering has little or no bearing on the issue" (recall, for example, my citation from Heschel, *Who Is Man?*); and dualism "asserts that the causal networks studied by the sciences and the realities attested by faith are both real but have nothing to do with each other."[17]

Farley's alternative is couched in Tillichian language: the biological is a dimension of human agency, or human personhood. He writes,

> The condition of human agents, whatever else it is, is the condition of living animals. The features that constitute life, animality, and being a mammal and a primate are not eliminated or left behind by whatever constitutes human agency. While it is the case that ciphers of transcendence such as self-presencing, love and evil are not simply terms for physiological states, it is important to remember that these things occur in conjunction with the living organism.[18]

While Farley's book differs from Hefner's in many ways, its basic flow is similar. A multidimensional interpretation of the human developed in the first part provides a basis for the second part, an account of sin and redemption. The religious symbols of the second part interpenetrate the account of the first for a Christian theological interpretation of the human condition. The scientific evidence crosses the intersection to theology, particularly theological anthropology, and deeply informs the theological interpretation. Human freedom is not simply interpreted as "spirit," somehow at least relatively independent from biology, but is accounted for within an account of scientific proposals. Farley does not draw out ethical implications for his synthetic account in specific ways, but the ethics would, I believe, necessarily be based upon the scientific information absorbed into the theological account of the human.

The intersection of science and theology, while it has renewed emphasis in current writings, is not novel historically, or even with reference to twentieth-century American theology. To catalogue bibliography in support of this generalization would be a historical project in its own right. However, the unique role of Ralph Wendell Burhoe and *Zygon*, a journal he founded and edited for many years (now co-edited by Hefner), needs to be noted. More than any other journal, *Zygon* has published articles by persons from various sciences who have significant interest in relating their work to religious and theological questions. The group closely associated with that journal has never developed consensus, but has been more consistently concerned to analyze, explore, and propose views which cross both directions of the intersection of theology and the sciences.

My examples have been from theologians; earlier in this chapter I posed another question: How do geneticists and other scientists move beyond the strict entailments of their investigations to explore the meaning and purpose of human life in what are religious affirmations or proposals, or at least the functional equivalents of them? This crossing of the intersection has been thoroughly analyzed and criticized by Mary Midgley in two books, *Evolution as a Religion: Strange Hopes and Stranger Fears* and *Science as Salvation: A Modern Myth and Its Meaning*. Midgley, particularly in *Science as Salvation*, interprets the speculations not only of biologists but also of physicists, astronomers, and others, and analyzes why they come to different conclusions in their "religious" or "theological" extrapolations and speculations. Her basic inquiry is to indicate how, in Gordon Kaufman's delineation of the theological enterprise, they "create a framework of interpretation which can provide overall orientation for human life."[19]

Efforts to extrapolate from biology or genetics, as well as from other sciences, to generalized interpretations of the "nature" of humans, society, and our place in the wider scheme of things has been a part of intellectual and social history for more than a century. These efforts have been chronicled not only by Mary Midgley, but by Richard Hofstadter, Carl Degler, and others.[20] Here I confine myself to one example, namely the great geneticist Theodosius Dobzhansky.

Dobzhansky, like others, is taken by a somewhat paradoxical point, an old one in Western thought, namely that by gaining more complete knowledge of the determinants of human and other forms of life, humans have the capacity (that is, it is part of their nature) to control life in the future. Biology gives knowledge, which in turn enables human beings to control, to determine, the future. The last pages of Dobzhansky's *Mankind Evolving*, which I first read about thirty years ago, are still memorable.

> Man has not only evolved, he is evolving. . . . Man is not the center of the universe physically, but he may be the spiritual center. Man and man alone knows that the world evolved and that he evolves with it. . . . [B]y chang-

ing the world in which he lives man changes himself. Changes may be deteriorations or improvements; the hope lies in the possibility that changes resulting from knowledge may also be directed by knowledge. Evolution . . . may conceivably be controlled by man, in accordance with his wisdom and his values.

This work ends with an ambivalent account of Teilhard de Chardin. Dobzhansky says that Teilhard's conclusion is not demonstrable by science, but that it "is not contradicted" by biological knowledge. It "comes as a ray of hope. It fits the requirements of our time."[21]

Dobzhansky is of particular interest because of his book, *The Biology of Ultimate Concern*, surely one of the most erudite attempts to relate modern biology to religion—indeed perhaps the only one by a biologist that shows serious study of religious thinkers. In a chapter titled "Search for Meaning," he says, "I do think that science, and particularly biology, are relevant to man's ultimate concern." Humans, even enlightened modern skeptics and agnostics, he says, "cannot refrain from at least secretly wondering about the old questions: does my life have some meaning and purpose over and above keeping myself alive and continuing the chain of living? Does the universe in which I live have some meaning, or is everything just a 'devil's vaudeville'?"[22] Again, as in the earlier work, Dobzhansky ends with a critical analysis of Teilhard that shows his ambivalence toward, but also his sympathy for, the poetic spiritual endeavor of the Jesuit.

The nature of the human has evolved so that we have capacities to "ethicize" (Dobzhansky's word), to think about the ends and means we will use as we participate in the evolutionary process. This seems to posit freedom as an aspect of human nature. Whether biology can fully account for the capacity to determine our ends is, of course, a currently debated question.[23] We have evolved so that we ask the meaning of life, and thus religion of some sort, or its functional equivalent, arises. The answers differ by biologists from a kind of Teilhardian inspiration to the famous conclusion of Jacques Monod: A human being "must realize that, like a gypsy, he lives on the boundary of an alien world; a world that is deaf to his music, and as indifferent to his hopes as it is to his sufferings or his crimes."[24]

Even the atheistic conclusion is given to fundamentally religious or theological questions. The nature of at least some humans seems to include a need to make judgments about life's meaning and significance, interpreted by looking at the human in a wide context of nature and culture, of which the human is a part. Biologists cross the scientific-theological intersection almost haphazardly when they seek to understand the fundamental nature of the human in relation to wider knowledge of nature, and proceed to interpret the significance of both the human and the wider context. Physicists and others cross the same intersection.[25]

Stephen Pope, Philip Hefner, and Edward Farley believe that contemporary sciences, particularly biology, must be taken into account in a theological interpretation of nature, and particularly the nature of humans. Traditional theology, however, keeps its independence, and thus biology is interpreted in the light of theology one way or another. Other writers, such as Ralph Burhoe, have been willing to jettison or radically reduce the authority of traditional Christian theology and its symbols. Dobzhansky's crossing of the intersection does not lead to traditional religious language about God and God's relations to the world, but he cannot let loose of the mystical interpretation of the sciences given by Teilhard de Chardin, whose conclusions, he says, are not demonstrable from science but are not incompatible with it. This seems to suggest a kind of parallel relationship: non-incompatibility warrants religious outlooks that are not necessary conclusions from the sciences.

For theology, I believe, the critical issues are the importance of "creation" and how it is explicated and becomes a basis for ethical norms and human values. A theology in which the second article of the Apostle's Creed is the most important approaches nature differently from one that accents the first article, belief in God as the "creator of heaven and earth." How God, the creator, is interpreted with reference to nature is the second important choice.[26] If nature or creation is of great importance, if not first importance, for theology, the interpretation of its processes and ordering comes not from religious myths but from current evidence, explanations, and interpretations drawn from works that focus on it scientifically.

❖ ❖ ❖

Theology per se has no independent access to the patterns and processes of nature. Stephen Pope's moves, I think, are correct. Furthermore, if morality is not only explained but in some ways justified by the theological ordering of nature (an argument for this conditional clause is not undertaken in this chapter), then theology is committed to a naturalistic basis for ethics. But this kind of project can occur only if the scientific-theological intersection is crossed both ways, that is, if sciences inform the understanding of nature that is interpreted theologically, and this interpretation becomes *a* (not *the*) basis for theological ethics, theoretical and applied.

❖6 *Human Viability:*
To What End?

Paul Ramsey's aphorism becomes a "text" one more time: "[Human beings] ought not to play God until they learn to be [human beings], and when they learn to be [human beings] they will not play God"![1] Then there are the words which the late Robert Morison, a science administrator and a major person in the development of "Science and Society" programs, spoke during a conversation about the points on which we agreed and disagreed: "I'm an atheist, but by God, I'm a Calvinistic atheist." My quoting Ramsey does not imply that I agree with his inferences from his aphorism; indeed, he consistently took a much harder line against various therapeutic experiments and medical procedures than I. Morison, I believe, was implying that for all of the developments of human capacities to influence the course of society, culture, and nature, *ultimately* they are not and will never be fully in human control, and thus his "Calvinism." But whatever is finally determinative is not necessarily beneficial to humans, to society, and to nature, and thus his atheism. My quoting Morison does not imply full agreement with him, either.

The theme of human viability is vast and multidimensional. If one sets it in the context of contesting cosmological hypotheses, one would have to choose which hypothesis is at this time most adequate. In most proposals, it seems to me, our galaxy as we know it is likely to end in the long-range future, and with it humanity, at least as we now know it. While one can draw inferences from such a view for religion and theology—for example, that belief in a divine goodness that ultimately is in focus on the human and its well-being and fulfillment is untenable—this is not the primary framework of this chapter.

If one sets the theme in the context of various scenarios about the sustainability of human life in the face of projected population growth, environmental depletion, escalating consumption, and the like, accountability for the future is more a matter of human individual and social choices. Specific inferences of relevance to theology and religion would depend to some extent on which scenario one is willing to adopt. One projection might lead to an alarming apocalyptic view; another might provide greater confidence in the human future.

Whether one chooses to reflect on the cosmological or the more impending ecological frame of reference, questions that have remarkably religious overtones are asked, implicitly at least, by both atheists and religious believers. In whom, or in what, can we have confidence, that is, "faith"? Whom or what do we not trust? To whom, or to what, are we faithful or loyal? For what can we hope? For what is it reasonable to aspire, or to expect? What evidence and support do we give to answers to these questions? As stated, these questions can be interpreted as global ones, involving the meaning and purposes of human activity in some ultimate way. But they are, I believe, answered implicitly in very particular choices made by individuals and centers of social power and authority, and shaped by various moral and cultural valuations. The answers have been, and continue to be, shaped also by the state of knowledge, life philosophies, and religious outlooks, as well as by personal dispositions and temperaments.

Faith and hope, approached in this way, are not uniquely religious. They are, as H. Richard Niebuhr describes, human phenomena, present in everyday experience as well as in the endeavors of science and other aspects of culture.[2] Confidence, faithfulness, and hope have "objects": persons, institutions, information, procedures of inquiry, purposes, ends, and so on. The faiths and hopes of persons are subject to descriptions and explanations that do not invoke a deity. Their apparent religious overtones do not, per se, make them religious in the restricted sense of convictions about and experiences of a power or powers that are the source of all that is, that bear down on us, sustain us, set an ordering of relationships of interdependence of things, provide the conditions of possibility for human activity, become a basis for ordering human conduct, and determine the final destiny of all that is.

If it will be granted that such a power, or powers, can be referred to by the word God—an assumption asserted rather than defended here—different ideas, sources, or experiences can be (and have been) used by religious thinkers to characterize God.

One can easily imagine that some theologians invited to discuss human viability would begin with biblical narratives in the confidence that they provide both a source (or even *the* source) of knowledge of God and a basis for projecting scenarios about human viability in shorter or longer runs of time. The prophets in the Jewish scriptures, for example, use extraordinarily vivid language to convey the utter destruction of the people who have betrayed their covenant with Yahweh and those who have destroyed Yahweh's people. But over and over they assure a future that is beneficial to the people, for example, "Though I have afflicted you, I will afflict you no more" (Nahum 1:12, NRSV). Inferences about the nature of God have been drawn from this historic assurance; God's grace and care surpass God's wrath and vengeance, and assure in the long run a human fulfillment beyond the suffering of history if not within history. No historic or natural threats to human viability can vitiate this ultimate faith and hope. There is a ground of confidence and hope beyond any scenario that proposes a tragic outcome for humanity.

Another theologian might begin with the biblical materials and use them as a basis for more complex inferences or speculations about the nature of God. For example, Jürgen Moltmann, in a chapter titled "God the Creator," asks these questions: "What does it mean for God to be the Creator of a world that is different from him, and is yet designed to correspond to him? What does this creation mean for God?" What is God's purpose with it? How does God experience it? I cannot recapitulate Moltmann's argument, but cite several of his conclusions. "God commits *himself* to create a world" with existential resolve of will and personal decision:

> Even "the end of the world" can set no limits to the God who has created the world out of nothing, the God who in his Son exposed his own self to annihilating Nothingness on the cross, in order to gather that Nothingness into his eternal being. And this is true whether the end of the world is brought about by natural catastrophe or human crime. Anyone who expects "the end of the world" is denying the world's Creator, whatever may prompt his apocalyptic anxiety. Faith in God the Creator cannot be reconciled with the apocalyptic expectation of a total *annihilatio mundi*. What accords with this faith is the expectation and active anticipation of the *transformatio mundi*. The expectation of "the end of the world" is a vulgar error. Anyone who believes in the God who created being out of nothing, also believes in the God who gives life to the dead. His faith makes him prepared to withstand annihilation, even when there is nothing left to hope for, humanly speaking. His hope in God commits him to faithfulness to the earth.[3]

Such a view does not rule out concern for the earth; indeed, it is part of Moltmann's project to establish the ground for ecological ethics, among other things. But by attending to the Bible and tradition and describing a view of God based on them as the first order of importance, he sustains the traditional Christian view that ultimate tragedy or despair are impossible, at least for the Christian believer.

The contemporary religious thinker who takes such assurances as these to be the ultimate truth about the destiny of the human and "world" will interpret and finally resolve issues in a certain way. If viability means not just survivability but also some fulfillment of qualitative well-being in own's own life, or in projections of the near future of human life, God does not fully guarantee it. Theologians, such as John Calvin, can enumerate the woes and afflictions of humankind with the starkest of realism, and even interpret them, as the prophets interpreted natural and historical events, so that God's purposes for the human, often hidden, are taking place through them. But there is assurance of an ultimate fulfillment. Whether the assurance of *ultimate* "viability" or fulfillment is given to a few or to all is a matter of particular doctrinal differentiation, but the general assurance that "God is for humankind," as Karl Barth iterates over and over, is the baseline for interpreting the human. In whom can humans have confidence? In God. To whom are they to be faithful? To God. For what can they hope? For a new creation of heaven and earth, even when there is nothing to hope for, humanly speaking. What are the grounds for this assurance? They are given in the biblical materials, and for Christians, particularly in the New Testament witness to Christ.

In order to interpret the historic, current, or future threats to human viability—whether that is thought of in terms of survivability or in terms of various indicators of human welfare and flourishing—a religious thinker who begins with this general perspective in one of its many forms has to render an account of these threats that does not deny the fundamental affirmation. In other words, from this perspective the ultimate beneficence of the Deity cannot be denied. But neither can the realities of threats to human well-being—well-being that is part of the divine beneficence. The historical options for the religious thinker are many, ranging from the starkness of views that affirm divine foreknowledge and foreordination, divine intention and action in every event—with providential meaning for humans—to the "secular theology" of the 1960s in which God had delegated the control of affairs to humans (who are just a little lower than the angels) to manage things. The options and arguments adduced in favor of one or the other view are not analyzed here.

Different impediments to human well-being that have to be taken into account include natural catastrophes such as earthquakes and epidemics, social structures and exercises of collective power, the outcomes of individual choices, and others. Differentiations are made about the extent of human accountability for each kind of threat or impediment. There has to be an analysis of both human capacities and human limitations: capacities to develop, for example, science and technology that enable increasingly significant interventions into the course of natural and social affairs; limitations that are due to what economists call "bounded rationality"—the absence of foreknowledge of outcomes and limits of control over them—and those due to some human fault, that is, the phenomenon of sin.

From this traditional and rather orthodox perspective, the question, In what and in whom we *ought not to trust?* is asked about the course of human events. It is asked about the uses of science, technology, and social power to change the course of history and even of nature. The answers are deeply ambivalent because they emerge from the ambiguous evidence about the reliability of human choices, individual and collective—and not only about specific choices, but also human desires—those that well up biologically and those that are shaped by culture and society. Even the most deterministic interpretations of the Deity as the decisive agent both in the long run of events and in particular events and actions find space for human accountability, for dimensions of the human spirit to be self-determining, and to have capacities to order events in the world in accordance with purposes and ends.

A plausible interpretation of Ramsey's aphorism might be that God has knowledge and power to determine the course of nature for the sake of human well-being. Human beings do not have such knowledge and power, and they err when they assume that they do. Their natural limitations, their bounded rationality and power (their "finitude," as theologians are wont to call it), and their deep tendency to have their hearts curved in upon themselves, their corruption, and sin, should be constraints upon their intentions and their actions.

Yet, I take it, while "progress" is not inevitable, in the course of modern history and culture human creativity and initiatives have relieved some human suffering and have developed activities that are beneficial to at least some segments of humankind. The human capacities for initiative and creativity are undeniable. The degree of confidence or mistrust that theologians have in these capacities depends on various judgments that are made, some of which are abstruse to the modern secular mind—such as the depth of the effects of the "fall" in the Genesis creation myths—some of which are assessments of human history that weigh the beneficial against the deleterious outcomes of human actions, and some of which reflect both religious and personal dispositions, for example, whether because of the divine goodness, novelty is to be grasped with openness, or because of human faults, one's primary attention is on the reality of possible evil outcomes and thus restraint. Judgments differ about whether that ultimate goodness of

God, which traditional Christian theology cannot deny, is a basis for confidence in human ends and activities, or is simply a symbol of a hope that, as Moltmann says, prepares humans to withstand annihilation even when there is nothing to hope for, humanly speaking. Do scenarios that describe serious threats to human survivability and human well-being count as evidence against the beneficence of the Deity in the traditional Christian perspective? No. Does confidence in the divine beneficence guarantee survivability and well-being during the course of human history? No, not absolutely, but it should engender out of gratitude and obedience a caring for human life and its qualities across all historic and social divisions of humankind.

I have attempted thus far to render a sketch of an outlook on the question of human viability from traditional and quite orthodox Christian theology. It is not one with which I agree, but it would be unfair not to have described it. If one wishes to represent, in some sense, theological ethics grounded in the Western religious traditions and expounded in Christian communities, a historic presumption is in their favor. A radical revision of theological ethics requires precise identification of the points at which one denies aspects of them, and the reasons for one's revision. That is a larger task than can be recapitulated in this chapter.

To sketch another alternative, also not fully my own, I now turn to the quotation from Robert Morison: "I'm an atheist, but by God, I'm a Calvinistic atheist." As I said previously, I cannot claim that I share Morison's reflections, but his words make a worthwhile starting point. In whom or in what can we have confidence, if this is a statement about some rather ultimate realities? Surely not in the beneficence of God, either in the short or the long run. Maybe in nature? The words seem to suggest a consent to natural powers that we cannot foresee to be in human control, but there is no decisive evidence that these powers are uniquely concerned with the survival or well-being of humankind. Should we trust in the accumulations of knowledge—scientific, humanistic, or what have you? Quite likely we should, to some degree, since knowledge enables humans to explain, interpret, and sometimes predict and control the outcomes of various activities. Thus knowledge can be used to guide actions based on human judgments about what ends are worthy or unworthy, what the limits as well as the possibilities of interventions are—with reference to some understandings of human well-being. Then, shall we place our confidence in human judgments about how various capacities and powers ought to be used? Probably we should, but in a qualified way. The venture of shaping the human future is increasingly in the capacities of those humans who have access to knowledge and the power to intervene into nature. The benefits of such human intervention have relieved many forms of human suffering, provided increased agricultural production to feed a growing population, restricted the effects of some epidemics, and so forth. But the same capacities have made possible the threats of mass destruction of persons and their living conditions through nuclear war, and continue to threaten human well-being and perhaps viability through the effects of the use of technology on the natural conditions necessary for well-being. The venture of giving ethical guidance to our shaping of the future in its basic natural, social, cultural, and personal conditions is necessary and worthwhile. Persons, and collectively institutions, are agents whose activities have outcomes for short- and long-range futures. But persons and institutions have interests that, in a classic Christian understanding of sin, are curved in on themselves, that limit their moral visions and constrict their moral sensibilities: economic interests, personal interests, political interests. And even the most well-intentioned interventions begin processes of interaction in societies and in nature that are beyond the control of the agents who introduce them.

We cannot hope for the transformation of the world in Professor Moltmann's terms. We cannot hope for the fulfillment of all justifiable human aspirations, in part because the belief that the "less perfect," that is, nature in all its forms, exists to serve the "more perfect" human is no longer plausible. That kind of anthropocentrism, backed as it was by Western thought in both religious and nonreligious forms, is not credible from this perspective. Nature, if one can be excused an anthropomorphism here, does not intend the well-being of the human as its final end, or telos; it does not guarantee that. Are we consigned to despair, not only with reference to some final end, if indeed despair is a necessary outcome of such a view, but also with reference to more proximate futures and ends?

Maybe the question "For what can we hope?" needs to be restated. For what can we reasonably aspire, given both the increased knowledge conditions which are the basis of increased control of various aspects of nature for human benefit and for destructiveness to human well-being? Can we hope for a sustained and sustainable world, while acknowledging that the course of events, which from some religious points of view was determined by divine providence, is not in critical ways determined by human choices and human actions? Does the outcome of Morison's Calvinistic atheism lead to resignation? Does it lead to vigilance about human activity? Resignation, from such a view, is not necessary; vigilance, caution, and humility are equally plausible outcomes. From both the starting points of either traditional Christianity or Calvinistic atheism, one comes to the circumstance of human capacities to be creative, to exercise powers in ordering the world, and to the ambiguities of outcomes of this exercise. Some of these are, in a sense, built into our finitude—constraints of foreknowledge and capacities to control the outcomes, and the necessity of dealing with probabilities rather than certainties.

A scenario something like this moved Hans Jonas to write about *The Imperative of Responsibility*, to search for an ethical basis for the technological age. Increased capacities to intervene technologically into the course of nature can lead to incremental consequences not foreseen and not intended which are deleterious in their outcomes, and for Jonas this warrants what he calls the "heuristics of fear."[4] He suggests that it is only when there are threats to human well-being, to "the image of the human," do we grasp the true image of the human. Only when we know *that* something is at stake for the human do we really know *what* is at stake. He claims that we are made in such a way that "the perception of the *malum* is infinitely easier to us than the perception of the *bonum*."[5] A similar meaning can be attached to Melvin Konner's quotation from Brecht's play *Life of Galileo*, "The aim of science is not to open the door to everlasting wisdom, but to set a limit on everlasting error."[6] In a sense these authors are saying that we achieve some increment in human wisdom as a result of human error; we achieve some understanding of human well-being and its necessary conditions as a result of the evil outcomes of human activities. Caution about technological interventions, and possible restraints or even reversals of activities, might follow from their "natural" consequences.

The critical judgment for Jonas, I think, is whether a threshold of irreversibility has been crossed. Robert Morison seems to have been saying that, while various malignant outcomes might be avoided, in the end the powers of nature will prevail over the wisdom of the human. Nature is God, perhaps, for Morison; the destiny of the human, even as it is deeply determined by human activities, is finally beyond the full control of humankind. And there is no guarantee that nature cares especially about human well-being. Such a view might lead to the previously quoted observation by Jacques Monod, that a human person "must realize that, like a gypsy, he lives on the boundary of an alien world; a world that is deaf to his music, and indifferent to his hopes as it is to his sufferings or his crimes."[7] Clearly this is a radically different view than one finds in traditional Christian theology.

I reiterate that whether one looks forward to a transformation of the world on some purely theological grounds, or to an ultimate indifference of nature to human well-being and survival, parties could agree that the capacities of humans to intervene in the course of nature are crucial. Whether beginning with traditional Christianity or Calvinistic atheism, we come to the issue of the human, its nature, its end, its trustworthiness. Ramsey's aphorism tells us that when we learn to be humans we will not play God. The aphorism carries the implication of a general prophetic warning, that humans ought not to assume what Ramsey apparently assumes about God, namely omniscience and omnipotence. The warning is fair enough; it reminds us of our finitude, our natural limitations. Morison's Calvinistic atheism has the same effect.

We come not only to the human, but to nature in a more inclusive sense as well. Is there a sufficient warning given to humans in the perceptions of the *malum*, the evil that occurs as a result of activity, for them to correct their course, to withdraw some interventions, and to reverse what are perceived to be evil effects? Does nature, or nature's God, provide at least a basis upon which human actions can be built, a basis (but not a sufficient one) for the ethics that will avoid potential catastrophes, if not guide humans and the natural world to greater well-being?

I turn now to these two issues—the human and the ordering of the natural world of which we are a part.

To be human is to be finite; it is not only to be consigned to death because of our mortal bodies, but also to have limitations of knowledge about life in the world and limitations of power to control the interactions that proceed from human interventions. Of course, the same limitations of knowledge and power do not pertain to every area of human activity; the predictive effectiveness of many interventions into nature are clear; the probabilities of achieving the end sought are high. But human viability and human well-being are affected not only by the "laws" of nature but also by the actions of human beings, and especially by the choices of persons and institutions with important economic, political, and other forms of power. In addition, it has become a commonplace to be suspicious of the knowledge of nature as masking limited perspectives and serving particular interests. By now most critical persons accept in general a view that our knowledge is conditioned by our perspectives and our interests, and that what we seek to know is subject to a variety of interpretations and meanings. And it is also clear that whether intended or not, the exercise of powers based on various forms of knowledge is governed in part by interests—moral, economic, political, and personal. Even if physical theorists come to agree on the mathematical formula that explains "everything," others will not find that useful to explain the particular times and places, circumstances and activities in which they are engaged. The lesson of human finitude, it seems to me, has been taught us well, and perhaps ad nauseam, in one set of terms or another.

The moral lessons to be learned from it, however, have not penetrated as deeply as one would expect. The moral lessons are the reduction of dogmatisms and the qualities of humility and tolerance that deter single-minded pursuit of narrow interests and the arrogance of absolute certainty in judgments of knowledge and morality. Ramsey's aphorism and Morison's Calvinistic atheism both back the importance of self-consciousness of limitations. They do not in themselves entail specific limits to interventions, though in practice Ramsey was more ready to do that than many persons have been.

I have already suggested in secular as well as in theological terms one of the outcomes of the finitude: limitation of knowledge and control, as well as contraction and restriction of valuations and interests, blinds us to knowledge we ought to consider, and hardens our hearts to the sufferings and the loss of conditions for the well-being of others. This is, in theological terms, sin. And this contraction or restriction is present in individuals, in collectivities, in institutions, and wherever most powers are exercised. This human fault is analyzed by secular as well as religious observers and interpreters. Because valuations and interests are matters not only of intellectual activity, but of our affections and passions (the heart, in traditional religious terms), the correction does not come simply by more adequate knowledge. The antidotes to the fault, the prescriptions of remedies are many: empathy for all sentient beings, identification with the poor and oppressed, vivid experiences of the effects of destructive forces caused by human beings, prophetic portrayals of apocalyptic scenarios through the heuristics of fear, and more.

Whether in secular or religious terms, there are calls for repentance based on remorse, for a change of heart and change of direction, for expansion of vision and affection. The preaching of repentance and the presumed correctives to this human fault occur from many secular and religious pulpits in the world. In religious language these are all calls for conversion of something: of our habits as consumers, our political views, our economic interests, our fundamental orientations toward the universe. Whether it is Gaia, the deity of process theology, or some new version drawing from the biblical traditions, whether it is the religious traditions rooted in Southern and Eastern Asia, there is a call to conversion to expand affections and interests.

Even those of us who deeply believe that the fault is a matter not only of brains but also of hearts cannot be sanguine about the effectiveness of such secular or religious rhetoric. Perhaps if the eightfold path of the Buddha, the teachings of Jesus, or the restoration of Gaia actually functioned we might see some significant change. But the limits are clear: rainforests are being depleted in traditionally Buddhist countries, and the marketplace functions as a major governance of life around the world rather than Yahweh, Jesus, or Gaia. There will be no conversion in a radical sense, at least not in the foreseeable future. Constriction of heart and mind continue. And thus we prudently work at smaller steps, using such powers as can be mastered to bring some controls to the effects of the driving forces of sinfulness.

Does nature, or nature's God, warn us of impending catastrophes sufficiently to avoid them? Karl Rahner, for example, believed that if humanity erred to the point of serious threats it would be turned toward some correction by the ordering of nature itself.[8] Hans Jonas seems to have some hope in the midst of his heuristics of fear that our perceptions of the evil outcomes of our activities will make clearer what is the human good and the good of the world. Certainly much of the evidence adduced for alterations both of interest and policies is drawn from the effects of our interventions into nature, whether in prolonging human dying, or in threats to environment. Morison's Calvinistic atheism seems to suggest that nature finally governs; one might infer from this that we ought to attend to its sighs to learn how better to govern ourselves and our activities. We do use "nature" as a basis, but not a sufficient one, for our ethics, willy-nilly.

This simply opens again in this book what is to me a most difficult intellectual issue that can be stated in theological or secular terms, that is, how do we justify reliance upon nature and knowledge of nature as bases for our ethics? In what senses are the forces and orders of nature norms from which we infer values and principles to guide our actions to avoid catastrophes if not fulfill human well-being? If we cannot finally trust and hope in humans because of their finitude and their constrictions of heart and mind, can we have confidence that nature or nature's God will keep humans in bounds by the apparently inevitable malefic outcomes of some of our activities? Is nature, or the ultimate power that has brought all things into being and will finally determine their destiny, a source of wisdom and strength so that, to play on the quotation from Brecht, we set a limit to everlasting error, if not open the door to everlasting wisdom? I offer an aphorism of my own. God (through nature) is the source of human good, but does not guarantee it. This does not cause apocalyptic anxiety, but it is not Moltmann's anticipation of a transformation of the world.

7 Conclusion: The Relations of Other Disciplines to Theological Ethics

The chapters of this book have been about intersections in one way or another, but that metaphor has not been exploited as it could have been. In different chapters different intersections have been in focus, and comparatively I have analyzed how the traffic meets if one is traveling different disciplinary or interest routes into it. In this concluding chapter I map out a more comprehensive pattern of traffic between other disciplines and theological ethics, drawing together discussions from previous chapters and adding some things not developed in them. Which disciplines intersect with theology or theological ethics and how the traffic is negotiated depend upon the interests of the scholar in those fields, as I have indicated, as well as on the theological and ethical assumptions and commitments that are held.

I have focused on some quite particular intersections, in which, for example, information from bioanthropology or genetics has to be taken into account; none of the chapters, however, is as "thick" or dense as, for example, environmental policy proposals. I have omitted more generalized issues of how moral philosophy as a discipline intersects with theological ethics, or how general epistemological and hermeneutical theories intersect with theology and theological ethics. My failure to attend to these crossroads does not mean that I consider them unworthy of attention. Works published by scores of proficient authors are both clarifying and interesting, and others are better prepared than I to work at the level of abstraction that is entailed. I am, however, convinced that high levels of abstraction often avoid some of the problems and some of the positive increments that occur when an intersection is descriptively dense.

The relations between moral philosophy and theological ethics, or Christian ethics, have been discussed for many generations of Protestant and Roman Catholic thought. The distinctions of Aristotelian and Thomist moral philosophy provided the framework for official Roman Catholic moral theology for centuries. With the development of phenomenology and personalistic philosophies, different relations were established by important contemporary authors. Arguments between "physicalists" and "personalists" were in part arguments about which moral philosophy best fit Christian theology and theological ethics, and what differences each makes in practical choices.

Protestantism has expressed the importance of this relation throughout its history, for example, in Melanchthon's use of Aristotle[1] and the impact of Immanuel Kant, Hegel, and other idealists. We have extensive discussions of the relations in influential twentieth-century literature, including Karl Barth's important passages in *Church Dogmatics* II/2, Paul Ramsey's use of the idealists Josiah Royce and Bernard Bosanquet in *Basic Christian Ethics*, Ian Ramsey's *Christian Ethics and Contemporary Moral Philosophy*,[2] and many other books and articles. As with debates between physicalism and personalism in Roman Catholicism, so in Protestant ethics, a shift in fashion of moral philosophy has led to changes in how philosophical ethical theory and

Christian ethics have been related. For example, the philosophical critiques of Enlightenment "universalism" has led to new interest in historical traditions and narratives and to certain Aristotelian themes; much theology now intersects with moral philosophy that represents those interests.

Observations about this are important for this book. First, the intersection of moral philosophy and theological ethics takes particular specificity depending upon which philosophies and theologies meet. The analysis, while having a common framework, would be quite different among important publications by persons I had the privilege to teach through the years. Gene Outka's *Agape* makes sophisticated use of the analytic moral philosophy dominant in British and American circles for some decades; it provides direction in which his version of Christian ethics flows. Stanley Hauerwas intersects with the "enlightenment project" in order to block its significance and finds a more complementary philosophical traffic in narrative and virtue theory. William Schweiker, in *Mimetic Reflections*, critically absorbs concepts and modes of analysis from phenomenological hermeneutics. William Spohn, a Roman Catholic, exploits the American tradition that flowers in the pragmatism of C. S. Peirce, G. H. Mead, and John Dewey to bring their interpretations of experience into Christian moral thought.[3]

Statements about science and theology make some general sense at a high level of abstraction, such as in epistemological issues; they become quite dense and require more specialized competencies and analyses when the focus is on, for example, quantum mechanics in relation to a doctrine of God, or evolutionary theory in relation to a doctrine of creation, or Freudian theory in relation to a theological interpretation of the person as moral agent. Analyses of the intersection of moral philosophy and theological ethics likewise depend upon which ethical theory is intersecting with which theological preference.

Different theological positions make one or another ethical theory either preferable or more and more alien. For decades I have pointed out how the biblical theological theme of "God acting in history" seems contrary to ethical theories that are rule dominated, and has more congeniality with ethical theories of "fitting" actions as found in stoicism and in pragmatism. A theological tradition with a practical focus on penance as part of its sacramental life needs a moral view that enables priests to number and grade the seriousness of sins; thus (at least at the practical level) moral theory of rules and a process of casuistry are developed.

I have not focused on the relations between moral philosophy and theological ethics in these chapters not because they are unimportant, but because they entail consideration of issues similar to those exposed in this book in a different range of literature.

My second observation is more substantial. Ethical theories propounded by philosophers have similar traffic patterns at similar intersections with other disciplines to those of theological ethics. One example has been noted, namely an ethical theory supporting the judgment that if it is immoral to use nuclear weapons it is immoral to threaten to use them. The presumption in this position is that one should move in one direction, from an ethical theory defended as the correct one in its own right, to the application of it to policies of deterrence. No analysis of comparative military strengths, of possible treaties and agreements and their enforceability, of political factors in nations involved would ever alter the authority of the theory; the autonomy of ethics is presumed and defended. Traffic flowed one way, though how it would merge with and affect the flow of military and political traffic is unclear.

Philosophical theories of ethics intersect with interpretations of the nature and activities of humans. Some descriptive premises are present in philosophical theories just as they are in theological views. Alan Gewirth, often characterized as one of the most rationalistic moral philosophers, builds his normative or prescriptive program of ethics on the basis of his understanding of the universal features of human persons: voluntariness and purposiveness.[4] About this one can ask, as I in effect did in chapter 1 about Reinhold Niebuhr's views, would the evidences adduced by Melvin Konner or E. O. Wilson in any way challenge or force alteration of voluntariness if not purposiveness? Could the genetic and bioanthropological evidence and interpretations we confronted at that intersection be absorbed as only further specifications of the "conditions" of action? Or, if the boundaries were open, would such interpretations require significant alterations of Gewirth's moral anthropology and thus affect both the content and form of his ethical theory? Or, for example, does recent physiological study of the brain imply that ethics of rules and their application run counter to natural processes which "explain" how we "know" other things; I heard a prominent philosopher so argue in a lecture. My inference from the lecture was that the "natural" way in which we gain knowledge is similar to Gestalt interpretations more than to some others; thus moral knowledge is gained in a similar way of relating parts to patterns, not unlike that proposed by John Dewey and H. Richard Niebuhr. The basic direction of traffic in this lecture was from scientific studies of the brain to a theory of ethics that was not only generated by that research but authorized by it.

Moral philosophers and theological ethicists, I observe, face the same intersections; thus matters developed in these chapters and matters that can be extrapolated from them have to be part of the agenda of philosophical ethics as much as theological ethics.

A third observation is that intersections such as those met in this book can be analyzed and discussed at very high levels of generality, or at densely descriptive levels. Given the current deep skepticism about the reliability or validity of the claims of the sciences as well as of social sciences and humanities, it is easy to focus on the presumed ideological bias from which an issue of intellectual or moral interest is framed, its information gathered, and its conclusions drawn. Various interests, economic and political powers, commitments to patriarchy and other repressive social organizations, and so on, are readily invoked not only to raise a critical perspective but also (in many instances) to dismiss the findings of a study or the proposals for a policy or moral course of action.

Much critical literature exists to proclaim the impossibility of pure objectivity in the interpretation of the meaning of biblical or other texts, in studies by historians and social and behavioral scientists, and even in studies by natural scientists. The relativization of claims that something objective to the knower is truly represented in what is claimed to be known about it is widely accepted. A whole range of positions run counter to the outcomes of these approaches, from hard realism to various qualifications of it which take into account the recent critical theories. My point here is that significant arguments can occur at a "meta-level," that is, at a very high level of generalization or abstraction. My point is also, however, that often at that level intellectual intersections become gridlocked—ideology versus ideology, or epistemological theories against each other.

When examining in detail some specific studies, whether historical, economic, literary, or physical, the analyst has to face precisely what has and has not been determined by the epistemological, political, or moral interest attributed to the author. Has certain information or data been ignored completely, for example, the role of women in a particular historical context? Is there agreement on relevant information, but difference in the attributed importance of aspects of it as causal factors? If, as often is the case, the overall scheme of interpretation is guided by a general perspective such as Marxism, can an alternative interpretation of the same events or circumstances demonstrate that the same information is susceptible to the alternative accounts? Many specific illustrations could be adduced to show that the denser an intersection is in its relevant information the more complex the argument becomes about the role of polarized ideological or philosophical frameworks. What can become traffic gridlocks (or in particular settings, shouting matches, polar position against polar position) can also become refined analysis of limited ways in which disagreements or misunderstandings occur, or ways in which mutual understandings and oftentimes mutual corrections occur. The analysis becomes "fine grained" because the materials cannot be reduced simply to being *determined* by an ideological or epistemological perspective.

None of this is to deny the importance and propriety of discussions at very general philosophical or ideological levels. It is, however, to propose that analysis of hermeneutical theories and the like requires attention to the ways in which the interpretation of specific texts or events are affected by different theories. Arguments about ethical theories, philosophical or theological, can go on without being imbedded in a thick description of a moral issue; that imbeddedness requires fine-grained analysis to sort out the effects of theories. Put a bit antagonistically, I have been exposed to very sophisticated and erudite discussions of methodological controversies in theology, theological ethics, history of religions, and other fields in which participants have never attempted to interpret a particular religious doctrine such as Christology, a complex moral or social problem, or the particular differences between Islam and Christianity.

As I have acknowledged, most of the material in the chapters of this book is not as dense in detail as it could be.

A major thrust of the book as a whole, however, is to show how detail, specificity, and density of material under analysis make the intersections between other disciplines and theology or theological ethics more complex than often is recognized. "Meta-approaches" can avoid the more complex, fine-grained analysis and bypass both specific issues of contention and specific possibilities of complementarity.

The remainder of this chapter draws on the previous chapters, as noted above, to frame an account of alternative ways in which other disciplines intersect theological ethics, and various ways in which the traffic is conducted. For organizational purposes, the intersections are expounded as themes.

In question form, the title of this chapter is: How do other disciplines relate to theological ethics?

The issues that emerge when we think about the relations of various disciplines to theological ethics are really a particular subset of issues that emerge when the same, or similar phenomena, are addressed by different academic fields or by different perspectives within the same fields. Recall, for example, the discussion in the introduction and chapter 1 about the human, its nature, its variety, and its activities. How do we negotiate between diverse descriptions, explanations, and evaluations of the human? Indeed, how do we identify what differentiates the human from other forms of life?

If we analyze comparatively such books as Abraham Heschel's *Who Is Man?*, E. O. Wilson's *On Human Nature*, G. H. Mead's *Mind, Self, and Society*, Gary Becker's *The Economic Approach to Human Behavior*, Jean Bethke Elshtain's *Public Man, Private Woman*, a postmodern novel like Don DeLillo's *White Noise*, or some classic dramas, Daniel Dennett's *Consciousness Explained*, Alan Donagan's *The Theory of Morality*, and others, there is an intersection that all these cross: the human, as species, as social groups, as gender groups, as individuals; and how human activities are described, explained, and interpreted, and implicitly or explicitly valued in some way. Different information, concepts, ideas, forms of argument, methodological and theoretical perspectives, and rhetorical styles intersect at the point where the human is the focus of attention. How do we negotiate between these diverse perspectives and contributions? How do we determine which approach is most adequate, or how do we find some operational coherence that suffices for whatever our purposes are? Recall Wayne Booth's words, "Must we not admit, then, in all honesty, that we are indeed a pack of ignoramuses, inhabitants of some ancient unmapped archipelago, each of us an island—let John Donne preach as he will—living at a time before anyone had invented boats or any other form of inter-island communication?" [5]

How various disciplines relate to each other when they cross the same intersection, then, is an increasingly difficult but important question in contemporary academic, cultural, political, and moral life. How various disciplines relate to theological ethics is only a particular subset of this larger experience. A basic assumption of this presentation is that no matter where each author or teacher is located on a map of theological ethics, no matter what claims each makes for its independent authority, for example, theological ethics necessarily engages in intersections with different nontheological, nonethical fields of research and writing. Thus implicitly or explicitly the choice of how other relevant disciplines relate to theological ethics is faced.

The relation of other disciplines to theological ethics is varied; here I only outline some possibilities. Which disciplines intersect depend upon the focus of attention in theological ethics. If one is concerned with moral anthropology, the human sciences from biology to the social and behavioral sciences have to be taken into account, or reasons given for ignoring them. If one is concerned with a theology of nature, and nature is a theological basis for ethics, physical sciences and biology will be more important than economics and sociology. If one is concerned to provide moral action guides, the disciplines that are most important for the arena of proposed action will come to the fore, such as economics, medicine, or international relations.

How one relates to various disciplines also varies with the theological and ethical assumptions or commitments one holds. If one works from a strong view of the authority of biblical revelation, one is likely to relate to various disciplines differently from a commitment to process theology. If a theology holds a historic theme such as love to be the defining characteristic of Christian ethics, it will be related to other disciplines differently from a natural law theory.

Before I delineate general themes of the relations, two hypothetical prefatory observations are in order, both of which are controversial. First, the nontheological discipline that many Christian ethicists use to cross into theological ethics is moral philosophy. As noted above, I do not attend to that here because I think that many of the issues and problematics one finds in crossing to theological ethics also occur when one moves from other disciplines to moral philosophy, for example, what constitutes an adequate moral anthropology.

Second, also as noted above, when one is negotiating the claims of disciplines that relate in various ways to theological ethics, general hermeneutical theories, general epistemological theories from extreme realism to extreme relativism, and general theories of the relations of facts to values, is to ought, are not very helpful. The issues that occur are finer grained; they are matters of judging the relative adequacy of closely related sources of information, and of explanatory arguments that are somewhat related to each other. One can criticize in general, for example, Gary Becker's utility maximizing view of both rational and irrational economic behavior with reference to certain assumptions about the scientific character of his work, to his behaviorist views of human action, and to his quantification of choices that others find reductionistic.[6] But all that is not sufficient to dismiss the predictive power of the probabilities he quantifies about average economic behavior. Indeed, many theologians have long avoided the harder issues of negotiating different, but relevant, information and explanations of activities presented in rigorous academic disciplines by relativizing them on the basis of general theories.

In the remainder of this chapter, I differentiate eight different themes about how other disciplines have been and are related to theological ethics.

Theme 1: Information, explanations, interpretations, and valuations from other academic disciplines *do not* cross the intersection to affect the substance of the theology or theological ethics. The sources and authority of theological ethics are independent from the human and other sciences that one finds in contemporary academic, public, and cultural life. The independence might be defended on the basis of special revelation as the authority and source, or on the importance of maintaining a distinctive historic tradition. But theology and ethics cannot be substantially altered by other disciplines.

One good example of this, already noted in chapter 1, is found in Rabbi Abraham Heschel's *Who Is Man?* For Heschel, the important question is who, not what, we are as humans. But "there is the ontological connective between human being and being human." What determines one's being human is the image one adopts "about human being." Heschel writes, "We can attain adequate understanding of man only if we think of man in human terms, *more humano*, and abstain from employing categories developed in the investigation of lower forms of life."[7] Responsiveness, a descriptive premise based on various sources including biblical, is the ground for the normative; we are to be responsive to ourselves, to others, and ultimately to God. Information and explanations from the human sciences, particularly those that demonstrate continuities between the human and other forms of life, are excluded from a theological moral anthropology.

This theme takes another version where an ethical principle, or moral value, is authorized on the basis of its biblical or traditional authority, such as the love command. Academic disciplines that argue that certain interpretations of that command, such as self-sacrifice, run counter to natural desires for happiness, and so on, might be denied as important. For example, I take the tension between some feminist writings on love, those of Stephen Post and Stephen Pope on the one hand, and on the other hand views of love typified (correctly or incorrectly is not our concern here) by Reinhold Niebuhr, Kierkegaard, and Gene Outka's *Agape* to be whether descriptive premises about self-sacrificial love derived from some human sciences and different human experiences should substantially alter the idea of love as a Christian moral norm.[8]

Theme 2: Information, explanations, interpretations, and valuations from other disciplines *pertain to the substance or content of theology and theological ethics*, and thus the intersection is crossed to require a revision of traditional theological and ethical theses. An example of this from history is the way in which Aristotelian science was used to describe and explain the workings of the Deity through nature in Thomistic theology, and thus ethics were grounded in and directed by the contemporary sciences of how humans really are—individually, communally, and as part of the whole order of creation.

I cite again the example of Philip Hefner's *The Human Factor: Evolution, Culture, and Religion*. Hefner attempts to stay within the boundaries of Christian orthodoxy and to take seriously contemporary philosophies of science, but also to use contemporary sciences as a source for understanding God and God's relation to the human through the ordering of nature. He writes, "The theological interpretation of what it means to be created is synonymous with the task of interpreting theologically the process of evolution, including the mechanisms of natural selection, which forms the conditioning matrix for human being."[9] In short, one interprets the evolutionary process as the work of God. The enormous task includes cosmology, the processes of development of physical reality, the biosphere, and human history and culture. Put oversimply, all of nature is God's great project. We understand the processes of this project from the sciences, though Hefner uses traditional theological themes to interpret their wider significance. But clearly the morally appropriate paths for humans are derived in large measure from God's great project, nature, interpreted by the sciences. The intersection has two-way traffic. Scientific disciplines inform theology quite substantially; the scientifically informed theology provides direction for the moral activities of persons, communities, and institutions.

Theme 3: Events described and explained by other disciplines *are redescribed and reexplained, or given additional meaning, from a theological ethical perspective.* The ethical follows from the theological redescription or reexplanation. In a sense Hefner's work uses this theme; it differs only in degree from the second. Different weights are given to how the sciences affect theology and ethics. Here I stress more the theological redescription, or a theological interpretation of the "meaning" of the scientific account.

This theme can be found historically in both popular and theologically sophisticated religion. The Puritans knew quite a bit about the secondary, or natural, causes of disasters, but they also interpreted them as omens of divine judgment or beneficence.

The theme also is found in many contemporary forms of liberation theology. Personal and historical narratives, statistical and other data, and analyses of structures of power are used to demonstrate the existence of dehumanizing and unjust racist, sexist, classist systems, relationships, and practices. In a sense, the oughts follow from the descriptive premises; the moral evil to be rectified is conceptualized by the descriptions and interpretations using nonreligious, nontheological concepts and language. But the ensuing account is also set in a larger religious or theological narrative: for example, that of salvation history which shows that God's will and action is liberation from various oppressions. What is, or can be, interpreted in terms of various academic disciplines, is redescribed, reexplained, and reinterpreted in religious moral terms, and even in quite direct theological terms. The events are not only political, but are what God is doing, such as humanizing. The proper moral action follows, in some way, from the theological interpretation.

Tensions exist within the same general theological ethical perspective about which descriptions and explanations are most appropriate to use in a theological and ethical reinterpretation. Feminist liberation writings, for example, agree on the general end of liberation from sexist oppression. There is argument, however, about what is the most appropriate description and explanation of the feminine, the masculine, and the universally human.[10] The chosen description makes a difference in the theological and ethical interpretation and in the moral outcome. Similar tensions within other generally agreed-upon aims of moral activity occur as a result of different judgments about what descriptive and explanatory accounts are to be accepted. The point to note here is this: materials from other disciplines that are selected for theological ethical redescriptions make both an ethical and religious difference. It also may be the case that the religious and ethical perspectives of the authors are a major selective factor in determining which descriptions are used.

Theme 4: Other disciplines provide the *descriptions and analyses of states of affairs, events, or persons to which Christian ethical principles are applied.* In this theme I wish to accent the application of ethical principles rather than a theological reinterpretation of the events.

Examples of this theme can be drawn from many writings on practical moral problems. In critical medical situations the circumstances are described and explained by medical science, and the range of choices from a moral perspective are framed by those accounts. Christian ethics then seeks to determine what love, or covenant fidelity, or regard for the alien dignity of the patient requires under the described conditions. In cases of military conflict, the circumstances in which noncombatant immunity is to be applied are described in terms of the hardware that is to be used, the enemy situations in which its use is proposed, etc., and a judgment is made about how the principle applies to these circumstances.

Most theologians would agree that the account is seldom morally neutral where states of affairs, events, or persons are described and explained in terms of relevant disciplines from the natural sciences or the social sciences. The language used, the factors accented or muted, and the configuration of information are all subject to overt or subtle moral bias. Thus descriptions by other disciplines are not approached with uncritical, naive confidence. At the same time, however, unless the ethicist commands the relevant technical knowledge, she or he remains dependent upon accounts provided by research done by others. An account of events or states of affairs that is not informed by the best knowledge available is as offensive as one that is patently skewed by the moral biases of the interpreter.

Theme 5: Other disciplines are *used to explicate a theological ethical viewpoint in nontheological, or operational terms.* Indeed, the intersection is often readily crossed both ways, or to change the metaphor, the boundary between theological ethics and other disciplines may be porous. But other disciplines function mainly *to make theological ethical claims intelligible* both to those within and outside of religious communities. The relationship is complementary or supplementary. A good example of this theme is James B. Nelson's 1971 book, *Moral Nexus*, which anticipated much of more recent discussion of how Christian moral identity is shaped by participation in the Christian church.[11] Nelson approached the formation of moral identity through the contemporary theories of socialization. Moral identity comes into being through socialization processes in particular communities. Christian moral identity is a particular instance of the general phenomenon. Two aspects have particular importance in that book: reference group theory and social role theory. The sociological and social psychological theories cohere with a relational view of the self, and with the theological ethics of Nelson's mentor, H. Richard Niebuhr. They provide an explanation of how Christian identity is formed in the context of social relations. As such the book also projects a practical blueprint of the necessary social conditions for the process to be effective. Something like the process Nelson depicts in social psychological terms is a necessary condition for religious narratives in Christian communities effectively to shape character and moral outlooks.

In this theme the traffic may be mostly one way: a theological ethical perspective is interpreted in scientific terms. Or it may be both ways: the social science (or in other examples, other sciences) coheres with theological ethics, and informs them, as well as theological ethics shaping a preference for a particular social science.

Theme 6: Theological ethics *might borrow authority from other disciplines* to add weight to its claims for ethical and even religious truth. We see this theme most often when a theological ethical position is judged to be wrong, often because it sustains practices and actions that can be judged to be immoral. Revision of theological ethics is authorized by information and analyses from nontheological disciplines.

An example of this procedure might be as follows. Within traditional theological ethics are imbedded descriptive premises drawn from hierarchical structures of domination; various forms of social oppression are religiously authorized. A prevalent example is the analysis and critique of patriarchy in the Bible and in subsequent Christian history. Patriarchy, a presumably culturally relative phenomenon, has gotten imbedded in the language and the practices of society and religious communities, against which are grounds for moral protest. Oppression and injustice ensue and are wrong. What is morally offensive is based upon incorrect descriptive premises in the theology and ethics—what might once have been called false views of the nature of the human. Given current investigations about the characteristics of humanity, and particularly about gender, new descriptive premises about the human have to be in place in the theological and ethical formulations themselves. Modern empirical data, whether the narratives of voices long silenced, or studies by biologists, social scientists, and others, require a revision of the theological and ethical premises. The authority of these sources is borrowed or used, in turn, to revise various aspects of ethical concerns: the priority of importance of various items on a moral agenda, the language in which any moral proposal is made, and the ends to be sought in moral activity.

This theme can also be illustrated from the reconsideration of the traditional morality of sexual relations. Modern knowledge drawn from various academic disciplines is used to argue that the relevant descriptive premises in the traditional religious and moral norms are false, or at least partial. New data, new explanations require not merely different applications of traditional norms, but different theological and ethical descriptive premises. These imply a reordering of values and a reconsideration of traditional norms.

Theme 7: When theological ethics are significantly affected by other disciplines, and when this leads to distortions of ethics, *one can seek to refute the other disciplines on their own terms*, that is, on basis of the data, explanations, and interpretations they have developed to establish their own authority.

This theme is not very evident in theological ethics. One finds it in the debates within various disciplines that might be used in theological ethics; one also finds it in debates between disciplines over, for example, the most adequate interpretation of the nature and activities of the human. Little of this is found in theological ethics simply because of the constraints that are present; theologians cannot become sufficiently schooled in the disciplines that relate to their work to make all the technical arguments required to refute a position, although general charges of "reductionism" are often heard. There are, however, some signs of this among writers of Christian ethics and economics. Different authors seek to undercut the data and theories that sustain their opponent's moral position by arguing the greater scientific adequacy of their own descriptive premises and explanations.

Theme 8: As stated, this theme might be broad enough to include all persons who are critically self-conscious of how they work in theological ethics. In the process of self-awareness of what premises are taken from other disciplines, *some general coherence is sought between theological and ethical premises and what is taken in, how it is interpreted, and how it is applied.* Ethicists do not want to rest their case completely on the truthfulness of information and explanations they use from other disciplines, but they would not have a case if the information and explanations did not have some reliability. One might want to insist for theological reasons on the independence of theological ethics with their own ground of authority, but at the same time make that position intelligible, if not justified, to those who hold it and to others who do not.

This framework of eight themes fulfills one purpose of this book, that is, to alert theological ethicists and their audiences to practices of their craft, especially in the context of the diverse contributions that many academic disciplines make to the field. Critical consciousness of both writers and teachers is (I hope) intensified. The framework also orders and to some extent expands a general theme of this book, namely the function and status of descriptive premises about nature, human beings, society, and events in theological ethics. The selection of various descriptive premises is a critical factor in theological ethics, no matter which theme dominates a particular book or article. All writers, teachers, and readers accept certain information, explanations, interpretations, and valuations as at least adequate for their various purposes. Many differences both in fundamental moral theology and in practical ethics are about the validity of descriptive premises and the explanations given them. The premises that are accepted make critical differences in shaping theological ethics in theory and in practice.

A quick reminder of this: recall various interpretations of moral agency, individual or collective. Reinhold Niebuhr's premises are different from H. Richard Niebuhr's; Lawrence Kohlberg's from Carol Gilligan's; Aristotle's from Kant's and Bentham's; Freud's from E. O. Wilson's; Rollo May's from B. F. Skinner's, etc., etc. Differences in descriptive moral anthropology have pervasive effects on every other aspect of theological ethics: for example, whether character and moral identity are more the focus of attention than discrete acts; the range and limits of self-determination and moral accountability; what features of agents are judged to be moral, premoral, or amoral; the explanations as well as justifications of moral choices; how sin is delineated; how grace affects moral action, and so on.

One might choose to avoid saying that the accepted descriptive premises are statements about the "nature" of things, as the references of that term have to be specified in different contexts. One remembers that Thomas Aquinas, among others, said with regard to humans that "nature" referred both to that which distinguished us from other animals and that which we shared with other animals. Explanations and justifications of particular moral actions in his moral theology often referred to both aspects of human "nature." Particular choices emerged from, followed from the descriptive premises of moral agents, of their relations to each other in community, and their relations to the wider world of institutions and nature.

Descriptive premises, whether they claim to represent nature or not, affect preferred choices of action. One may, or may not, like to think that theological ethics are "naturalistic" in some strong or weak sense, that the morality which emerges or follows from a theological ethics is heavily dependent upon various descriptive premises used. But the weight of analyses in this book is that they do, whether one wishes to admit it or not.

This is clearer and more rigorously the case in ethical matters that draw upon the natural sciences than those that draw upon other disciplines. I noted medical choices earlier; choices about environmental ethics are more ambiguous but nonetheless have some inchoate sense of a dynamic equilibrium of natural and technological forces that might prevent disastrous outcomes. But the decisive impact of descriptive premises is also readily seen in alternative proposals for health care, education, political economy, the reduction of violence, family life, and so on.

Here we come again to issues that systematically follow from this and previous chapters, issues only named here. First, what concepts or metaphors should be used in accounts of the importance of descriptive premises for our understanding of ourselves as agents or our circumstances of choice? Does what we value flow from, emerge from, follow from the descriptive premises? Are our values anchored in, based upon, or dimensions of these premises? Do they supervene them? Et cetera.

If I have plausibly established ways in which other disciplines are related to theological ethics, and their importance in providing information, explanations, interpretations, and evaluations that we use, then it behooves writers and readers to think very carefully and systematically about answers to these questions. A point developed above deserves repetition: how we think about these matters when dealing with particular studies that make fine-grained connections is not satisfactorily resolved by general hermeneutical theories, general epistemological theories, or general theories of relations of facts to values.

A Coda

Intellectual, academic, and practical problems and interests in our time fit less and less the traditional divisions of the academy. Biologists, chemists, and physicists intersect in shifting cohorts as issues emerge which no one discipline has the information, the concepts, or the explanations to explore. One can hear or read what are nearly jeremiads and at least puzzled self-examinations of particular disciplines, such as anthropology, as the attempts are made to determine their distinctiveness, their comprehensiveness, and their relations as receivers and contributors to other academic work. What information should be used? What hypotheses and theories should be explored? What revisions of established directions and boundaries of research and writing should occur? These and other questions are asked in part because what attracts our attention and interest, intellectually and morally, expands or breaks the boundaries of customary ways of thinking and acting.

As scholarly fields, theology and theological ethics are not exempt from these conditions unless they are isolated by choices of their participants. The subjects examined and positions proposed necessarily intersect the contributions of other fields. They can provide critical perspectives on the contributions of others, but they are also open to critical examinations from the perspectives and work of others. Theology and theological ethics have no grounds on which to be the critics of other fields if they do not permit work from other fields to be critical of them. They should be undefensively open to justifiable revisions as they and other disciplines intersect on common interests or problems.

Finally, not only theological scholars and teachers in educational institutions are in intersections; pastors and parishioners are as well. Some writers propose disengagement of the church from cultural, social, intellectual, and moral intersections, in part to find the particularity from which the church or Christians can prophetically critique the world. I cannot grasp the meaning of such proposals in other than the most artificially abstract terms. My observation is that a significant portion of clergy and other Christians appreciate an honest and forthright analysis of how intersections in which they live and think can be interpreted and maneuvered through. Biblical language and terms are not the first language most Christians use to interpret or explain events, or even to articulate what they mean. At least some persons are puzzled by the fact that they speak psychology, biology, sociology, politics, or economics as the appropriate language to understand most events and relations while at the same time believing (in some sense) that religious or biblical language is really the most adequate. The task of understanding and directing traffic of information and ideas, including religious, in the intersections of much ordinary human experience is one for the churches as well as the academy. The intellectual demands are at least as important in the congregations as they are in the academy.

Notes

Preface

1. James M. Gustafson, review of Howard R. Bowen's *Social Responsibilities of the Businessman*, in *Christianity and Society* 19, no. 1 (winter 1953–54): 21–23.

2. James M. Gustafson, *Ethics from a Theocentric Perspective*, 2 vols. (Chicago: University of Chicago Press, 1981 and 1984). For Farley's comment, see Harlan Beckley and Charles Swezey, eds., *James M. Gustafson's Theocentric Ethics* (Macon, Ga.: Mercer University Press, 1988), 39–40.

3. James M. Gustafson, "In the Intersections: Reflections on Being an Academic Traffic Cop," *Criterion* 14, no. 1 (winter 1995): 7–14.

4. Wayne Booth, *The Vocation of a Teacher* (Chicago: University of Chicago Press, 1988), 316.

5. See D. Bruce Johnsen, "The Formation and Protection of Property Rights among the Southern Kwakiutl Indians," *Journal of Legal Studies* 15 (1986): 41–67. I am indebted to Professor Peter Aranson of Emory's economics department for calling attention to this article during a seminar titled "Describing, Explaining, and Valuing."

Introduction

1. James M. Gustafson, *Treasure in Earthen Vessels: The Church as a Human Community* (New York: Harper and Bros., 1961).

2. Jürgen Moltmann, *God in Creation* (San Francisco: Harper and Row, 1985), 197–214; Freeman Dyson, *Infinite in All Directions* (New York: Harper and Row, 1988), 288–99; Philip Hefner, *The Human Factor: Evolution, Culture, and Religion* (Minneapolis: Fortress Press, 1993), 33–41.

3. James M. Gustafson, *Varieties of Moral Discourse* (Grand Rapids, Mich.: Calvin College and Seminary, 1988); Gustafson, *A Sense of the Divine: The Natural Environment from a Theocentric Perspective* (Cleveland: The Pilgrim Press, 1994).

4. See "What Is the Normatively Human?," reprinted in James M. Gustafson, *Theology and Christian Ethics* (Philadelphia: United Church Press, 1974), 229–44.

1. Explaining and Valuing the Human: An Inevitable Theological and Scientific Encounter

1. Reinhold Niebuhr, *The Nature and Destiny of Man*, 2 vols. (New York: Charles Scribner's Sons, 1941 and 1943), 1:1; Melvin Konner, *The Tangled Wing: Biological Constraints on the Human Spirit* (New York: Harper Colophon Books, 1983), xi; Carl Degler, *In Search of Human Nature: The Decline and Revival of Darwinism in American Social Thought* (New York: Oxford University Press, 1991), 3. Hereafter references to these works by Niebuhr and Konner will be cited with page references in the text.

2. For a discussion of this, see Jean Bethke Elshtain, *Public Man, Private Woman*, 2d ed. (Princeton, N.J.: Princeton University Press, 1993), 228–55.

3. Abraham J. Heschel, *Who Is Man?* (Stanford, Calif.: Stanford University Press, 1965), 16. Emphasis in original.

4. Ibid., 3.

5. Edward O. Wilson, *On Human Nature* (Cambridge: Harvard University Press, 1978), 2; Wilson, *Sociobiology* (Cambridge: Harvard University Press, 1975), 3.

6. Wilson, *On Human Nature*, 208, 209.

7. Mary Midgley, *Beast and Man* (Ithaca, N.Y.: Cornell University Press, 1978), 253–83, for her discussion of alternatives to football match polarization.

8. Gary Becker, *The Economic Approach to Human Behavior* (Chicago: University of Chicago Press, 1976). Becker's book is discussed further in subsequent chapters.

9. Hans Jonas, *The Imperative of Responsibility* (Chicago: University of Chicago Press, 1984); Joseph Fletcher, *The Ethics of Genetic Control* (Garden City, N.Y.: Doubleday Anchor Books 1974).

2. Moral Discourse about Medicine: A Variety of Forms

1. For an interesting, informative account of casuistry, its history and current importance, see Albert R. Jonsen and Stephen Toulmin, *The Abuse of Casuistry: A History of Moral Reasoning* (Berkeley: University of California Press, 1988).

2. Ivan Illich, *Medical Nemesis: The Expropriation of Health* (New York: Bantam Books, 1977), front cover.

3. Ibid., 32–33.

4. Ibid., 91–92.

5. J. Grant, trans. and ed., *Selected Political Speeches of Cicero* (New York: Penguin Books, 1969), 97.

6. Leon Kass, *Toward a More Natural Science: Biology and Human Affairs* (New York: The Free Press, 1985), 101–2.

7. Ibid., 113.

8. Ibid. On pp. 310–11, Kass describes other features and potentialities that he values, e.g., "Through moral courage, endurance, greatness of soul, generosity, devotion to justice—in acts great and small—we rise above our mere creatureliness, for the sake of the noble and the good" (p. 311).

9. Jose M. A. Delgado, P*hysical Control of the Mind: Toward a Psychocivilized Society* (New York: Harper and Row, 1969), 223.

10. For two forceful arguments against prophetic utopians, see Melvin J. Lasky, *Utopia and Revolution* (Chicago: University of Chicago Press, 1976), and Jonas, *The Imperative of Responsibility.*

11. The most prominent proponent of this view in Protestantism is Stanley Hauerwas; his most systematic book to date is *The Peaceable Kingdom: A Primer in Christian Ethics* (Notre Dame, Ind.: University of Notre Dame Press, 1983). His many essays on issues of medical care reflect this perspective.

12. Renée C. Fox and Judith P. Swazey, *The Courage to Fail: A Social View of Organ Transplants and Dialysis*, 2d rev. ed. (Chicago: University of Chicago Press, 1978), 135–79; quote from p. 179.

13. Melvin Konner, *Becoming a Doctor: A Journey of Initiation in Medical School* (New York: Penguin Books, 1987).

14. Gene Outka, "Social Justice and Equal Access to Health Care," *Journal of Religious Ethics* 2 (1974): 11–32.

15. In part these reflections stem from social roles I have had as a sometime member of the advisory committee to the director of the National Institutes of Health, and of the board of a major not-for-profit health system in the Chicago area.

3. Styles of Religious Reflection in Medical Ethics

1. Mary Midgley, *Heart and Mind* (Brighton, U.K.: The Harvester Press, 1981), 131. Emphasis in original.

2. Arthur Danto, *Mysticism and Morality* (New York: Harper Torchbook, 1972); Joseph Kitagawa, *The History of Religions* (Atlanta: Scholars Press, 1987), 246.

3. Edward Shils, "The Sanctity of Life," in Daniel Labby, ed., *Life and Death* (Seattle: University of Washington Press, 1968), 3, 12, 18–19, 38.

4. Midgley, in Harlan Beckley and Charles Swezey, eds., *James M. Gustafson's Theocentric Ethics* (Macon, Ga.: Mercer University Press, 1988), 193.

4. Genetic Therapy: An Intersection of Science, Ethics, and Theology

1. See the following articles, published over a decade: W. French Anderson, M.D., and John C. Fletcher, Ph.D., "Gene

Therapy to Human Beings: When It Is Ethical to Begin," *New England Journal of Medicine* 303 (27 November 1980): 1293–97; Anderson, "Human Gene Therapy: Scientific and Ethical Considerations," *Journal of Medicine and Philosophy* 10 (1985): 275–91; "Human Gene Therapy: Why Draw a Line?," *Journal of Medicine and Philosophy* 14 (1989): 681–93; and "Genetics and Human Malleability," *Hastings Center Report* 20 (January/February 1990): 21–24.

2. One example of this literature is Daniel Bergsma, ed., *Ethical, Social and Legal Dimensions of Screening for Human Disease* (New York: Stratton Intercontinental Medical Book Corp., 1974).

3. Anderson and Fletcher, "Gene Therapy to Human Beings: When It Is Ethical to Begin," 1295. See also Anderson, "Human Gene Therapy: Scientific and Ethical Considerations," 278.

4. Anderson, "Human Gene Therapy: Scientific and Ethical Considerations," 283.

5. Ibid., 285.

6. Ibid., 285–87.

7. Ibid., 288.

8. Anderson, "Human Gene Therapy: Why Draw a Line?," 687.

9. In Kass, *Toward a More Natural Science,* 157–86.

10. Anderson, "Human Gene Therapy: Why Draw a Line?," 687. See also p. 689 of same article, and Anderson, "Genetics and Human Malleability," 24.

11. Anderson, "Human Gene Therapy: Why Draw a Line?," 689.

12. Ibid.

13. Anderson, "Genetics and Human Malleability," 24.

14. Anderson, "Human Gene Therapy: Scientific and Ethical Considerations," 286.

15. Anderson, "Human Gene Therapy: Why Draw a Line?," 689.

16. Anderson, "Human Gene Therapy: Scientific and Ethical Considerations," 286.

5. Theology, Biology, and Ethics:
Further Explorations

1. For a fuller analysis of this issue, see Peter D. Browning, "Genetic Intervention: A Theological and Ethical Response" (Ph.D. diss., University of Chicago, 1987).

2. Paul Ramsey, *Fabricated Man* (New Haven, Conn.: Yale University Press, 1970), 138.

3. Karl Barth, *Church Dogmatics* III/4 (Edinburgh: T. and T. Clark, 1961), 397–470.

4. Wilson, *On Human Nature*, 2.

5. Ramsey, *Fabricated Man*, 139–40; Karl Rahner, *Theological Investigations*, 23 vols. (New York: Herder and Herder, 1972–96), 9:205–24, 225–52, 215–16.

6. Ibid., 219.

7. Ibid., 211–12.

8. Ramsey, *Fabricated Man*, 38, 31.

9. J. Robert Nelson, *Human Life: A Biblical Perspective for Bioethics* (Philadelphia: Fortress Press, 1984), 130.

10. Wilson, *On Human Nature*, 208.

11. Karl Barth, *Church Dogmatics* III/2 (Edinburgh: T. and T. Clark, 1960), 71–202; Heschel, *Who Is Man?* 3.

12. Barth, *Church Dogmatics*, III/2: 198, III/4: 200, 202.

13. Troeltsch, in Robert Morgan and Michael Pye, eds., *Ernest Troeltsch* (Atlanta: John Knox Press, 1977), 117; Paul Tillich, *Systematic Theology* (Chicago: University of Chicago Press, 1963), 3:5.

14. For a discussion of Burhoe and others see Hefner, *The Human Factor*, 93.

15. Stephen J. Pope, "The Ordering of Love in Recent Roman Catholic Ethics: A Constructive Proposal," *Theological Studies* 52 (1991): 278–79. This article is drawn from Pope, "The Contributions of Contemporary Biological Anthropology to Recent Roman Catholic Interpretations of Love" (Ph.D. diss., University of Chicago, 1988). See also Pope, *The Evolution of Altruism and the Ordering of Love* (Washington, D.C.: Georgetown University Press, 1994).

16. Hefner, *The Human Factor,* 60, 75, 81.

17. Edward Farley, *Good and Evil: Interpreting the Human Condition* (Minneapolis: Fortress Press, 1990), 78.

18. Ibid., 79.

19. Midgley, *Evolution as Religion: Strange Hopes and Stranger Fears* (London and New York: Metheun, 1985), and *Science as Salvation: A Modern Myth and Its Meaning* (London and New York: Routledge, 1992); Gordon D. Kaufman, *Theology for a Nuclear Age* (Philadelphia: Westminster Press, 1985), 26. On Midgley's work, see also my review article, "Scientific Dreamers and Religious Speculation," *Christian Century* 110 (10 March 1993): 269–74.

20. See Richard Hofstadter, *Social Darwinism in American Thought,* rev. ed. (Boston: Beacon Press, 1955); Degler, *In Search of Human Nature;* Hans Jonas, *The Phenomenon of Life: Toward a Philosophical Biology* (New York: Dell Publishing Co., 1960).

21. Theodosius Dobzhansky, *Mankind Evolving* (New Haven, Conn.: Yale University Press, 1962), 346–47, 348. Cf. the quotations from Troeltsch and Tillich above (note 14).

22. Dobzhansky, *The Biology of Ultimate Concern* (New York: The New American Library, 1967), 94, 98.

23. This is an issue in current brain/mind debates. See, for example, Daniel C. Dennett, *Consciousness Explained* (Boston: Little, Brown, 1991).

24. Jacques Monod, *Chance and Necessity* (London: Fontana Books, 1974), 160.

25. See, for example, Freeman Dyson's Gifford Lectures, among many more delivered under that auspices, *Infinite in All Directions.*

26. I have not here discussed the interesting example of Moltmann's *God in Creation,* 1985, which finds a happy concurrence between God as Spirit, the physical theory of the expanding universe, and an eschatology of hope.

6. Human Viability: To What End?

1. Ramsey, *Fabricated Man,* 138.

2. See H. Richard Niebuhr, *Faith on Earth: An Inquiry into the Structure of Human Faith* (New Haven, Conn.: Yale University Press, 1989).

3. Moltmann, *God in Creation,* 72, 80.

4. Jonas, *The Imperative of Responsibility,* 26–27, 204–6.

5. Ibid., 27.

6. Konner, *The Tangled Wing,* xvi.

7. Monod, *Chance and Necessity,* 160.

8. Rahner, *Theological Investigations* 9:217.

7. Conclusion: The Relations of Other Disciplines to Theological Ethics

1. For Melanchthon's use of Aristotle, see "Commentary on Aristotle's Ethics, Bk. 1," in Ralph Keen, trans., *A Melanchthon Reader* (New York: Peter Lang, 1988), 179–201.

2. Karl Barth, *Church Dogmatics* II/2 (Edinburgh: T. and T. Clark, 1957); Paul Ramsey, *Basic Christian Ethics* (New York: Charles Scribner's Sons, 1950); Ian Ramsey, ed., *Christian Ethics and Contemporary Philosophy* (New York: Macmillan, 1966).

3. Gene Outka, *Agape* (New Haven, Conn.: Yale University Press, 1972); Stanley Hauerwas, *A Community of Character* (Notre Dame, Ind.: University of Notre Dame Press, 1981), and many other books and articles; William Schweiker, *Mimetic Reflections* (New York: Fordham University Press, 1990); William Spohn, work in progress at the time of this writing.

4. Alan Gewirth, *Reason and Morality* (Chicago: University of Chicago Press, 1978), 21–42.

5. Wayne C. Booth, "The Idea of a University—as Seen by a Rhetorician," in *The Vocation of a Teacher,* 316.

6. See Becker, *The Economic Approach to Human Behavior.*

7. Heschel, *Who Is Man?* 16, 8, 3.

8. Cf., e.g., Barbara H. Andolsen, "Agape in Feminist Ethics," *Journal of Religious Ethics* 9 (1981): 69–83; Stephen G. Post, *Christian Love and Self-Denial* (Lanham, Md.: University Press of America, 1987); Stephen J. Pope, "Expressive Individualism and True Self-Love: A Thomistic Perspective," *Journal of Religion* 71 (1991): 384–99; and Outka, *Agape.*

9. Hefner, *The Human Factor,* 42.

10. See, for example, Elshtain, *Public Man, Private Woman;* and Elizabeth Fox-Genovese, *Feminism without Illusion* (Chapel Hill: University of North Carolina Press, 1991).

11. James B. Nelson, *Moral Nexus: Ethics of Christian Identity and Community* (Philadelphia: Westminster Press, 1971).

Bibliography

Anderson, W. French, M.D. "Genetics and Human Malleability."
Hastings Center Report 20 (January/February 1990): 21–24.

———. "Human Gene Therapy: Scientific and Ethical Considerations." *Journal of Medicine and Philosophy* 10 (1985): 275–91.

———. "Human Gene Therapy: Why Draw a Line?" *Journal of
Medicine and Philosophy* 14 (1989): 681–93.

Anderson, W. French, M.D., and John C. Fletcher, Ph.D. "Gene
Therapy to Human Beings: When It Is Ethical to Begin." *New
England Journal of Medicine* 303 (27 November 1980):
1293–97.

Andolsen, Barbara H. "Agape in Feminist Ethics." *Journal of Religious Ethics* 9 (1981): 69–83.

Barth, Karl. *Church Dogmatics*. II/2. Edinburgh: T. and T. Clark,
1957.

———. *Church Dogmatics*. III/2. Edinburgh: T. and T. Clark, 1960.

———. *Church Dogmatics*. III/4. Edinburgh: T. and T. Clark, 1961.

Becker, Gary. *The Economic Approach to Human Behavior*. Chicago:
University of Chicago Press, 1976.

Beckley, Harlan, and Charles Swezey, eds. *James M. Gustafson's
Theocentric Ethics*. Macon, Ga.: Mercer University Press, 1988.

Bergsma, Daniel, ed. *Ethical, Social, and Legal Dimensions of Screening for Human Disease*. New York: Stratton Intercontinental
Medical Book Corp., 1974.

Booth, Wayne. *The Vocation of a Teacher*. Chicago: University of
Chicago Press, 1988.

Browning, Peter D. "Genetic Intervention: A Theological and Ethical Response." Ph.D. diss., University of Chicago, 1987.

Danto, Arthur. *Mysticism and Morality*. New York: Harper Torchbook, 1972.

Degler, Carl. *In Search of Human Nature: The Decline and Revival of Darwinism in American Social Thought*. New York: Oxford University Press, 1991.

Delgado, Jose M. A. *Physical Control of the Mind: Toward a Psychocivilized Society*. New York: Harper and Row, 1969.

Dennett, Daniel C. *Consciousness Explained*. Boston: Little, Brown, 1991.

Dobzhansky, Theodosius. *The Biology of Ultimate Concern*. New York: New American Library, 1967.

―――. *Mankind Evolving*. New Haven, Conn.: Yale University Press, 1962.

Donagan, Alan. *The Theory of Morality*. Chicago: University of Chicago Press, 1979.

Dyson, Freeman. *Infinite in All Directions*. New York: Harper and Row, 1988.

Elshtain, Jean Bethke. *Public Man, Private Woman*. 2d ed. Princeton, N.J.: Princeton University Press, 1993.

Farley, Edward. *Good and Evil: Interpreting the Human Condition*. Minneapolis: Fortress Press, 1990.

Fletcher, Joseph. *The Ethics of Genetic Control*. Garden City, N.Y.: Doubleday Anchor Books, 1974.

Fox, Renée C., and Judith P. Swazey. *The Courage to Fail: A Social View of Organ Transplants and Dialysis*. 2d rev. ed. Chicago: University of Chicago Press, 1978.

Fox-Genovese, Elizabeth. *Feminism without Illusion*. Chapel Hill: University of North Carolina Press, 1991.

Gewirth, Alan. *Reason and Morality*. Chicago: University of Chicago Press, 1978.

Gustafson, James M. *Ethics from a Theocentric Perspective*. 2 vols. Chicago: University of Chicago Press, 1981 and 1984.

―――. "In the Intersections." *Criterion* 14, no. 1 (winter 1995): 7–14.

————. "Scientific Dreamers and Religious Speculation." *The Christian Century* 110 (10 March 1993): 269–74.

————. *A Sense of the Divine: The Natural Environment from a Theocentric Perspective.* Cleveland: The Pilgrim Press, 1994.

————. *Theology and Christian Ethics.* Philadelphia: United Church Press, 1974.

————. *Treasure in Earthen Vessels: The Church as a Human Community.* New York: Harper and Bros., 1961.

————. *Varieties of Moral Discourse.* Grand Rapids, Mich.: Calvin College and Seminary, 1988.

Hauerwas, Stanley. *A Community of Character.* Notre Dame, Ind.: University of Notre Dame Press, 1981.

————. *The Peaceable Kingdom: A Primer in Christian Ethics.* Notre Dame, Ind.: University of Notre Dame Press, 1983.

Hefner, Philip. *The Human Factor: Evolution, Culture, and Religion.* Minneapolis: Fortress Press, 1993.

Heschel, Abraham J. *Who Is Man?* Stanford, Calif.: Stanford University Press, 1965.

Hofstadter, Richard. *Social Darwinism in American Thought.* Rev. ed. Boston: Beacon Press, 1955.

Illich, Ivan. *Medical Nemesis: The Expropriation of Health.* New York: Bantam Books, 1977.

Jonas, Hans. *The Imperative of Responsibility.* Chicago: University of Chicago Press, 1984.

————. *The Phenomenon of Life: Toward a Philosophical Biology.* New York: Dell Publishing Co., 1960.

Kass, Leon. *Toward a More Natural Science: Biology and Human Affairs.* New York: The Free Press, 1985.

Kaufman, Gordon D. *Theology for a Nuclear Age.* Philadelphia: Westminster Press, 1985.

Kitagawa, Joseph. *The History of Religions.* Atlanta: Scholars Press, 1987.

Konner, Melvin. *Becoming a Doctor: A Journey of Initiation in Medical School.* New York: Penguin Books, 1987.

————. *The Tangled Wing: Biological Constraints on the Human Spirit.* New York: Harper Colophon Books, 1982.

Labby, Daniel, ed. *Life and Death.* Seattle: University of Washington Press, 1968.

Mead, G. H. *Mind, Self, and Society.* Chicago: University of Chicago Press, 1934.

Midgley, Mary. *Evolution as Religion.* London and New York: Metheun, 1985.

———. *Heart and Mind.* Brighton, U.K.: Harvester Press, 1981.

———. *Science as Salvation.* London and New York: Routledge, 1992.

Moltmann, Jürgen. *God in Creation.* San Francisco: Harper and Row, 1985.

Monod, Jacques. *Chance and Necessity.* London: Fontana Books, 1974.

Nelson, J. Robert. *Human Life: A Biblical Perspective for Bioethics.* Philadelphia: Fortress Press, 1984.

Nelson, James B. *Moral Nexus: Ethics of Christian Identity and Community.* Philadelphia: Westminster Press, 1971.

Niebuhr, H. Richard. *Faith on Earth: An Inquiry into the Structure of Human Faith.* New Haven, Conn.: Yale University Press, 1989.

Niebuhr, Reinhold. *The Nature and Destiny of Man.* 2 vols. New York: Charles Scribner's Sons, 1941 and 1943.

Outka, Gene. *Agape.* New Haven, Conn.: Yale University Press, 1972.

———. "Social Justice and Equal Access to Health Care." *Journal of Religious Ethics* 2 (1974): 11–32.

Pope, Stephen J. *The Evolution of Altruism and the Ordering of Love.* Washington, D.C.: Georgetown University Press, 1994.

———. "Expressive Individualism and True Self-Love: A Thomistic Perspective." *Journal of Religion* 71 (1991): 384–99.

———. "The Ordering of Love in Recent Roman Catholic Ethics: A Constructive Proposal." *Theological Studies* 52 (1991): 278–79.

Post, Stephen G. *Christian Love and Self-Denial.* Lanham, Md.: University Press of America, 1987.

Rahner, Karl. *Theological Investigations.* Several vols. New York: Herder and Herder, 1972.

Ramsey, Ian, ed. *Christian Ethics and Contemporary Philosophy.* New York: Macmillan, 1966.

Ramsey, Paul. *Basic Christian Ethics.* New York: Charles Scribner's Sons, 1950.

———. *Fabricated Man.* New Haven, Conn.: Yale University Press, 1970.

Schweiker, William. *Mimetic Reflections.* New York: Fordham University Press, 1990.

Starr, Paul. *The Social Transformation of American Medicine.* New York: Basic Books, 1982.

Tillich, Paul. *Systematic Theology.* Vol. 3. Chicago: University of Chicago Press, 1963.

Wilson, Edward O. *On Human Nature.* Cambridge: Harvard University Press, 1978.

———. *Sociobiology.* Cambridge: Harvard University Press, 1975.

Index

tonomy and intelligibility,
57, 68–72
dignity: as background condition, 83, 93; as belief condition, 77; ethics of ends
and, 91
disciplinary context, 27–28,
57, 146–47; additional
meaning from theologi-
cal ethical perspective,
138–39; affecting sub-
stance of theology or theological ethics, 136–37;
application of ethical principles and, 139–40; bor-
rowing authority from
other disciplines, 141–42;
descriptive levels of intersections, 130–33; disciplinary intersections with
theological ethics, 133–
46; ethical theories and,
129–30; intelligibility of
theological ethical claims,
140–41; refuting the dis-
tortion of ethics, 142–43;
relations between moral
philosophy and theological
ethics, 127–29; reliability
of information from other
disciplines, 143; revision
of traditional theses,
137–38; themes of,
136–46
distributive justice, 53
DNA research, 15, 73, 94
Dobzhansky, Theodosius,
106–8
doctrine of God, 6–7, 100

doctrine of particular revelation, 59–61, 66–67
Donagan, Alan, 133
Donne, John, 134
double effect, principle of, 79
dualism of body and soul, 21,
104
Dyson, Freeman, 7

Eastern Orthodoxy, 60
Eastern religions, 67
ecological ethics, 114, 145
*Economic Approach to Human
Behavior, The* (Becker), 27,
133
economic theory, 27, 135–36
Elshtain, Jean Bethke, 133
empirical tradition, 23–24
ends: ethics of, 91; morality of,
65
enhancement therapy, 76,
78–81, 84–85, 96
Erikson, Erik, 33
Essay on Man (Pope), 20
ethical discourse, 37–41
ethical theories, 38–39, 75,
87, 128–30
ethics, 52; authority of, 1–4,
99; autonomy of, 57–62,
87; ecological ethics, 114,
145; formulation of ethi-
cal issues, 74–84; intelligibility of, 62–72, 140–41;
nature as basis for, 124–
25; refuting distortion of,
142–43. *See also* medical
ethics; religious ethics;
theological ethics
ethics of ends, 91